MW00324380

RASCAL
AND ME

A Voyage Around the Eastern
U.S. and Parts of Canada Alone

RASCAL AND ME

A Voyage Around the Eastern
U.S. and Parts of Canada Alone

Phil Phillips

Rascal and Me, copyright © 1999, 2021, Phil Phillips.

All rights reserved. No part of this book may be reproduced or transmitted in any form or by any means, electronic or mechanical, including photocopying, recording, or by any information storage and retrieval system, without permission in writing from the copyright owner.

Cover images: © iStockphoto: kbwills; DepthofField; sara_winter, all rights reserved.

Paperback ISBN: 978-0-578-99870-1
Originally published by Xlibris, 2005,
hardcover ISBN: 0-7388-0582-3 and
paperback ISBN: 0-7388-0583-1
LCCN 99-91017 // V.2.0

This book was printed in the United States of America.

Additional copies of this book and two more books by the author, *Fast Boat Nekkid* and *Slow Boat Nekkid*, are available from Amazon and other fine retailers.

Contents

This book is dedicated, to Grant Edward Phillips, a mariner in the making, who at age ten has already accompanied his father seaward along the south coast of Florida and across the Gulf Stream into the Bahamas, to Mary Kathryn "Kitty" Phillips, my wife and best friend of many years, to Kathleen T. "Tommie" Phillips, of indeterminate age, and to Philip B. Phillips, M. D., who with Tommie started all this.

Acknowledgments

WRITING A FIRST BOOK, I have learned, is anything but a solo venture. It is a team sport in which the most important player, aside from the writer himself, is the editor. It was my serendipitous good fortune to have my editor move from California to become my next-door neighbor. We met and became friends. The only error of judgment I have observed him make came when he agreed to help me with this project. Aside from being a smart guy with an educator's grasp of the language, he is a veteran boater, contributing editor of the *Waterway Guide,* and as genial and good natured a man as there ever was. Tom Fryer deserves much of the credit for the success of this book. I remain responsible for its shortcomings.

No doubt the word processor is the CB radio of the 90s, but I never owned a CB radio *or* mastered the word processor, so I elected to write the first draft of this book the old-fashioned way, in longhand in spiral notebooks stowed in *Rascal's* small cabin. Each evening, no matter how exhausted, I would write of the day's experiences and every week or so, send these pages by facsimile to my office. There Tina Hatlee, using a word processor, would transcribe my scribbling into orderly, typed pages. Later, working together, we edited the manuscript time and time again before turning the whole thing over to Tom Fryer for his master strokes.

An early draft was sent to some friends for their comments. Charles Palmer and Jack Burnell responded extensively as did George Bedell, himself a writer and retired book publisher. Their thoughts led to improvements and their encouragement inspired me to keep working.

The many people I met along the way unwittingly made valuable contributions of their own: they gave each place I visited a special texture and context all its own. Two such people stand out in my memory, perhaps because I was with them longer. They are the brothers, Alan and Brian McKenzie, of the Village of Argyle in Nova Scotia. I number them among my friends. But there are so many others. People who offered aid in distress or lent a hand when I needed a hand or volunteered information—the "local knowledge" that is the mother's milk of boaters and without which the hazards of unfamiliar waters can become life-threatening. To all of them, my heartfelt thanks.

Preface

THIS BOOK IS AN ADVENTURE story and a travelogue. It is the story of my 7,661-mile, three-month circumnavigation of the eastern United States and parts of eastern Canada in a small boat, alone. The route I followed is known among boaters as the Great Circle Route. Among non-mariners, it is not generally known that the entire eastern third of the United States can be circumnavigated.

The book will appeal to these audiences: first, to men and women who take pleasure from human dramas born of extreme personal peril. Second, to restless souls who feel their lives lack excitement and challenge. Third, to those who enjoy sea stories with their mix of fate and danger, struggle and misfortune, fear and survival. Fourth, to travelers by land or sea, who will venture into areas I visited along the Great Circle Route. These travelers will find useful material on things to see, places to stay, and a few memorable watering holes. Finally, to any mariner who contemplates a similar circumnavigation, this book should be of significant assistance. As for places to stay, I have included the names of individual establishments only when the place was noteworthy, or particularly well located.

A theme of this book is man's old and intimate relationship with sea and land. For travel, commerce, exploration, or, as in my case, for solitude and sheer adventure, waterways offer splendid possibilities.

Yet for family, shelter, safety, and rest, man returns to his home ashore. This book is about both land and sea and the separate loves I have for each.

While much of the book describes experiences on my voyage—weather, seas, cities, towns, landscapes, seascapes—some of it is concerned with glimpses of the history of places visited. My choices of the parts of a place's history to include reflect entirely my own interests and philosophy and may annoy serious historians or local inhabitants for what is ignored or treated lightly. Similarly, some readers may take exception to one or more of the personal points of view I express on issues that arose in the course of my journey. Again, the opinions reflect my beliefs and world view. By all means, feel free to disagree.

Other parts of this book describe people I came to know along the way, mostly people engaged in an enterprise of one sort or another. I talk about what they do for a living, how they came to do it, and why they do it well. My affection for them will be apparent.

Coastal travel that begins in the Deep South and passes northward along the shores of New England exposes the traveler to two (there are more) distinct cultures. Even a casual observer cannot help but notice the differences between these regions. Speech, architecture, sense of community, self-expression, and attitudes toward liberty and order vary widely. I reflect upon these differences and try to understand why they exist and what created them. In doing this, I have borrowed from two important works. The first, a *tour de force* of Americas founding cultures, is *Albion's Seed* by the gifted scholar David Hackett Fischer, Warren Professor of History at Brandeis University. The second, more focused on the South, is *Cracker Culture* by Grady McWhiney, Lyndon Baines Johnson Professor of American History at Texas Christian University.

Throughout this book, I have used an unusual literary convention. I left on this voyage from my home port of Jacksonville, Florida, standing at the helm of a boat I had named *Rascal*, a sleekly shaped vessel built of fiberglass with a few stainless steel parts and adornments. I returned safely aboard a friend. Somewhere along the way, after this boat had rescued me from fear and disaster more times than I can guess, *Rascal* had become my trusted friend. I had for the first time in my life formed a bond of affection with an inanimate object. *Rascal* was no longer "it" but, in the tradition of the sea, had become "she." Reflecting on this, I have used the unconventional "we" throughout this book to mean *Rascal* and me. "I" is used only where the action involved is my own. Two other conventions of lesser note: I have tried to use only such nautical terms as can be understood from their context in order to make the book more accessible to readers without extensive boating experience, and the miles I refer to are statute, not nautical.

What follows is an account of a personal adventure.

ONE

Big Decisions

I'M BORED. My bountiful, blessed, repetitive life has grown stale. I have spent the most recent twenty-two years of my adulthood earning a living, the last ten of these also raising a family. After some trying years, facing financial ruin, my business now thrives. Best of all, it almost runs itself. The people who work for me are skilled and do their jobs far better than I could and without supervision. I am not superfluous to my business; neither is it critical that I be at my desk every day.

I am not lost, just stuck. The electricity has been turned off. I feel no animating passion, and passionlessness is an unnatural state for me. I long to take risks again, confront obstacles, face danger. I miss the exhilaration, to borrow Winston Churchill's phrase, of being shot at without result. I want to reawaken my wilder spirits.

No longer a believer in needless exertion or personal discomfort, I rule out any activity to achieve this goal that is likely to result in excessive perspiration. "No pain, no gain" is somebody else's motto, not mine. This rules out hiking the length of the Appalachian Trail, or biking across America, or climbing Mt. McKinley. My years as a soldier and student have given me quite enough experience, thank you very much, with deprivation. Sleeping uncomfortably, especially on hard ground, eating bad food, or eating any food without agreeable wine will not be part of the plan. Clearly these self-imposed limitations restrict available options. It is the rare adventure that is accompanied by sound sleep, good food, and decent wine.

I consider the possibility of a steamy affair with a gorgeous young thing. Quickly my imagination runs into a brick wall, for two reasons. First, my wife will not welcome this solution. Period. Second, no second reason is needed. There's always the option of a safari in Africa, or a trip to Antarctica, or a cruise around the world. These ideas interest me little. I've done enough traveling by common carrier to know that it lacks the risk, the implicit danger I'm looking for. I've never much enjoyed being an ordinary tourist anyway.

Walking along the beach near my home in northeast Florida one early spring day I consider the question of what I might do. The broad expanse of the Atlantic Ocean lies before me, its white- caps as restless as I am. Lost in thought, I see a boat pass, its wake cutting a bold line across the aquamarine sea, and it comes to me all at once. I'll take a long trip by boat, somewhere. I have been around boats since my boyhood in Pensacola, and I'm a competent, if somewhat rusty, seaman. I could travel on a boat to places I've never seen.

Time is not a serious limitation. With fax machines, cell phones, and overnight delivery, I can manage my business from anywhere for about as long as I choose to be away. Inevitably, there would be perils to be faced: threatening seas, storms, fog, tricky navigation, mechanical failure. It all sounds wonderfully appealing. I am convinced. With little hesitation, I decide I will take a long boat trip. Somewhere.

As I walk along the seashore stepping more briskly now, I begin to consider possible destinations and what kind of boat I'll need. Just last year, I took my 31-foot outboard south along the coast from Jacksonville to Stuart, then headed up the St. Lucie River, across Lake Okeechobee (second to Lake Michigan, the largest freshwater lake in America), down the gorgeous Caloosahatchee River to Fort Myers and the Gulf of Mexico, then around Florida's Big Bend and its "Redneck Riviera," and from there west and south across Alabama, Mississippi, Louisiana, and Texas, all the way to the Mexican border at Brownsville. It had been a fine, long trip—more than a thousand miles—but it was far from the ultimate adventure.

I had used the same boat and others I have owned to cruise to South Florida, Bimini, the Florida Keys, and the Abaco Islands in the Bahamas. These were relaxing trips, none longer than a few weeks. Except for two harrowing crossings of the Gulf Stream between Florida's east coast and the Bahamas Bank, they were not memorable, mostly vagrant wanderings on flat, transparent waters over spectacular coral reefs. I would not return to these places on this trip. I am not seeking relaxation.

How about Argentina? I could run from Florida down the Caribbean islands all the way to the South American coast. This idea lacks originality in a large yacht; it's been done many times before. But I could do it in my outboard or some other small boat. How would I get the boat back? Running it back would take too long, or would it? I could sell it down there and fly home. If I head south in the summer, when I'd hope to go, there could be hurricanes and tropical storms to contend with, and I seek danger, not doom. Perhaps I should ship my boat to San Diego and cruise the California, Oregon, and Washington coasts north to British Columbia, maybe even Alaska. Or how about shipping it to Europe and circumnavigating the Mediterranean Sea? As I walk along the shore, smelling the salt air, I am excited just to imagine the possibilities. I return to my truck parked a few miles down the beach and drive home, splendidly exhilarated.

In the following week, I reach some decisions. Europe and California are too far away for now; planning for them would be too time consuming. I want to leave soon. They'll make good places for second and third trips. The Caribbean, though instinctively my first choice, is problematic. In a large boat, it could be a fairly routine cruise, lacking challenge. A small boat could find itself constantly in uncomfortable seas, especially below twenty degrees latitude, because of the strong prevailing southeasterly trade winds. Seas would be on the port beam, not the ideal place for a small boat to be slammed by big waves.

My thoughts turn north. Quickly I decide this is the direction I will go. I have never been north of St. Simons Island, Georgia, by water, so it will be new territory. The Intracoastal Waterway (ICW) offers a protected, if sometimes troublesome, passage nearly all the way to New York City. Beyond that point, other decisions will be needed, but these can wait for now. Weather will be a key factor, and, as always with weather, timing is crucial. Leave too soon and cold and fog will be a problem early in the trip. Leave too late and cold and storms could strike late in the voyage. The weather window will be small, thus the length of the trip will depend on the speed I can average.

I think about a boat. There is no real mystery to the physics of boats. The larger the boat, either the slower it will go or the more power and thus more fuel it will take to push it through the water at a given speed. This principle is generally valid in powerboats regardless of hull type or design. Boats grow larger as they are called on to perform more functions. Thus, equipping a boat with a stateroom and head, however compact, will require more room and thus more power than a boat without these amenities. Add a galley and saloon, and the boat grows larger still. To maintain a given speed, its engines grow too, along with the size of the space required for the engine (or engines). The potential for mechanical failure increases geometrically as systems grow larger and more complex.

In boat selection, the single most important concept to master is *compromise*. So, I must first consider what functions I want a boat to serve on this trip most of the time, recognizing that no boat will perform all functions all of the time. Because of the short weather window, speed is important. It's also important because going fast creates its own excitement. By eliminating as many functions as possible, I can greatly enhance speed, and I can eliminate most of these functions by the simple expedient of relying on shore-based facilities. If I eat in local restaurants, sleep in motels, and dock the boat at marinas, I won't need a galley or stateroom or saloon or maybe even an enclosed head. Stopping each night will allow me the chance to socialize with the locals and thus learn more about an area, eat well, and sample local foods, not to mention that it will free me from the tasks of cooking and cleaning.

For most of the trip, I choose to travel alone. All of us spend nearly all of our lives in social settings—family, work, school, clubs, friends, sports. These require constant interaction with others. Anthropologists tell us that humans are the animal kingdoms masters of social skills. Except when we sleep, we are constantly interacting with others. Throughout my life, I have never really been alone. Now for a time, I want to experience solitude, to be away even from those I love. I want to be utterly free from the need to accommodate myself to others or to be accommodated by them. I will make all decisions without consultation or advice—and I will suffer or rejoice in the consequences. I will know whom to hold responsible if things fall apart and whom to praise when all goes well. The price for this temporary self-indulgence is the absence of a companion with whom to share events. It is a price I am willing to pay, at least for a time.

Traveling alone, I will have the opportunity for sustained introspection. At mid-life, I want time to think about the second half. If I end the pursuit of economic gain in a few years—a likely decision—in what direction should I go? Philanthropy? Bluewater sailing? Teaching? Golf? Can I really walk away from the challenges of competitive commerce and enjoy leisure as a way of life? These are serious questions and they require thoughtful reflection. It will be useful to consider them in fresh settings far from the places and routines of my daily life.

My dear wife, Kitty, is successfully busy with her own profession and with nurturing our ten-year-old son, Grant, Master of the Universe. As a devoted mother, she has the good sense not to take potentially life-endangering risks. Nor do I want her to. We agree that her presence onboard would not be good for either of us. Grant is far too young for the journey. Kitty has long known of my desire for adventure, my wanderlust. The trip comes as no surprise to her. To her credit, she encourages me to go.

There are also practical reasons to travel alone. A smaller boat, such as I am considering, when loaded with voluminous charts and cruising guides, foul-weather gear, duffel bags packed with clothes for both hot and cold weather, and all the paraphernalia required for long-distance cruising, leaves little room for a second person's gear and, with their gear included, no room at all for one person, let alone two, to sleep aboard if necessary. Anyone going along would have to limit themselves to a part of the trip, and even here there are problems. Coordinating rendezvous and departure points is often a boater's nightmare. A meeting place can usually be settled easily, but arrival time can be unpredictable by days or weeks because of the uncertainties of travel by boat. For this trip, the correct number of travelers is one.

I need to make a final decision about where I will go. The ICW will take me almost to New York City. From there, I have roughly three choices. I can run up the Hudson River to a point just north of Albany and there take the Erie Canal west across New York to Lake Ontario, continuing the trip from there. I can run up the Hudson through Lake Champlain and the Richelieu River to the St. Lawrence River and up the St. Lawrence to Montreal, continuing from there. I am drawn to the third alternative: leave the city, head out Long Island Sound, along the Connecticut shore, through the Cape Cod Canal, and up the coasts of Massachusetts, New Hampshire, and Maine.

The first two choices would make interesting travel but lack an essential feature. They are in mostly protected waterways. There is too little open ocean and the risk and exhilaration that go with it. I eliminate the first two tracks and focus on the third, but it, too, needs improvement. It is too short. I calculate that I could reach Maine easily in three to four weeks, and I want this trip to last two to three months. So I need to address questions of distance and time.

With a map of the eastern U.S. and Canada in hand, and making some assumptions about average boat speed and miles traveled per day, I begin to calculate how far I could go in an allotted time of, say, two months. I schedule time at various places for extended layovers—extra days in Charleston, New York, Martha's Vineyard, and Boston. But wait, I remind myself This trip is not a race. I need to subordinate my Type A compulsiveness for a moment-by-moment itinerary, leaving time to cruise slowly in beautiful places, to stroll through appealing towns, to luxuriate under sunny skies. A schedule that's too inflexible will have me on a treadmill. In fact, as I reflect further, I will not have a schedule at all. I will leave a place on a day and at an hour that seems fitting at the time or, in other words, whenever I please. Time will, for once in my life, be my servant, not my master. Now that this is decided, I can forget about how long the trip will take. It will take as long as it takes.

Returning to the question of where I'm going, I study the map and a route begins to suggest itself From Maine there is little alternative except to enter the Bay of Fundy and cross it somewhere to Nova Scotia. Arriving at Nova Scotia, the only choice is to traverse its east shore to the Gulf of St. Lawrence. At this point the question arises whether a) to continue north to Newfoundland, cross the Gulf and enter the St. Lawrence Seaway or b) to round Nova Scotia, make the passage between the mainland and Prince Edward Island, and hug the Gulf's south shoreline to the mouth of the St. Lawrence. I worry that getting fuel in the remote parts of Newfoundland will be a problem, so I focus on the Gulf shoreline as the route to the St. Lawrence. At that point, it's up the St. Lawrence River to Lake Ontario, where other choices present themselves. I can take the Welland Ship Canal into Lake Erie and beyond or take the Trent-Severn Waterway literally over the mountains to the Georgian Bay, a part of Lake Huron, and from there into Lake Michigan or Lake Superior.

I call my chart supply store, Bluewater Books in Ft. Lauderdale, and order some large planning charts and a few cruising guides. I talk to a knowledgeable salesman about the possibilities. He says much of Lake Erie is ugly and rusty industrial. He suggests I take the Trent-Severn, a canal of 240 miles with forty-four locks, some quite unusual. Immediately, I reject the Lake Erie option and choose the Trent-Severn instead, undaunted by the large number of locks. From the Georgian Bay, I can cruise the North Channel to the mouth of the St. Mary's River which flows out of Lake Superior, past Sault Ste. Marie, and into

Lake Huron. From here I can cross into the main body of Lake Huron and pass through the Straits of Mackinac into Lake Michigan.

I like it. And I'm beginning to get very excited about all this. I can run down Lake Michigan to Chicago and into the Illinois River, across the state of Illinois, into America's mightiest river, the Mississippi, above St. Louis. Down the Mississippi, at Cairo, Illinois, I can take the Ohio River upstream to its junction with the Tennessee near Paducah, Kentucky. Here I can make my way into the Tennessee-Tombigbee Waterway that will take me through parts of Kentucky, Tennessee, Mississippi, and Alabama into the Gulf of Mexico at Mobile. By now, I can barely contain my energy; my blood is up. I want to do it! Today!

I quickly fly to Fort Lauderdale, to Bluewater, and get plenty of useful tips from the folks there. I buy a massive collection of charts, large ones for planning purposes and conventional ones for navigation, covering the entire route from Jacksonville to Maine, around Nova Scotia, all the way to Mobile. Then I decide, as I like to decide, impulsively, what the heck, once I'm in Mobile, I can run the south and west coasts of Florida to the southernmost city in the country, Key West, then up the east coast to home. Wow! That would be a complete circumnavigation of the whole eastern U.S. and parts of Canada, more than seven thousand miles. It is a route with everything I'm looking for. I buy still more charts and a big stack of cruising guides and have everything shipped to my office. No way can I get this mass of material on the plane with me.

Back home, with the route chosen, I turn my attention to boats. I've already decided the boat does not need a galley, stateroom, saloon, or enclosed head. It will need a dry, lockable storage area where I can keep personal gear, charts, and other essentials.

The route will take me through remote areas where there may not be motels, certainly not near any harbors. I may also choose to anchor out in remote places overnight. Both of these possibilities mean the boat, though it will not need a stateroom, as such, will at least need a dry place where I can sleep and a small, portable head. A cuddy cabin will serve. I must be prepared for dirty weather. I will surely encounter rain, wind, and fog. Threatening seas are likely. And cold. The boat must offer protection from these and, above all, it must be seaworthy in rough water.

I had always supposed that I would need to buy and equip a new boat for this trip, but now, after carefully reviewing all the requirements, I begin to consider the boat I already own. It is a thirty-one-foot Fountain, an open boat with a cuddy cabin forward, and a center instrument console covered overhead with a canvas T-top mounted on a tubular frame above the helm. It is powered by two 225-horsepower Mercury outboards.

It is a fine boat but deficient in several important respects. The T-top over the console and the windscreen are inadequate for protection against harsh weather. Its big outboards are gas guzzlers and, with a single 207-gallon fuel tank, its range, with a reasonable margin for error, is only about two hundred miles. Refueling considerations are significant. Most importantly, it is a light, fast boat, open to the sea and weather. I think it may be too small and too light for the seas of the North Atlantic. The experienced sailors I talk with all agree. They suggest a deep-keel sailboat of at least thirty to forty feet or a stout motor yacht—a big, heavy, ponderous boat but reassuring in bad weather. It doesn't take long to figure that on such slow boats, I would be deep into winter before I could get out of the Great Lakes. And, for an excitement seeker, the idea of chugging along all day on such a painfully slow boat is not appealing, the thought of owning one even less so.

Slowly, I begin to see the beauty of taking the boat I already own, named *Rascal*, despite her shortcomings. She is very fast. Flat out she runs sixty, and fast cruising speed is just over forty. To achieve these speeds, she must plane, running on top of, rather than through, the water. She is an extremely sound, seaworthy boat with an offshore race-bred deep-vee hull that performs well in rough water and performs better the faster she runs. Off plane, she's a cork. And therein lies the problem. If the seas should get so grisly that it's impossible to run on plane—not likely, but possible—I could get into serious trouble. On the other hand, her speed allows me to get out of the way of storms, to reach safe harbors quickly.

Finally, after much agonizing, looking at other boats, talking to experienced sailors, and exhausting my analytical faculties, I decide that my boat will serve the purposes I wish to put her to about as well as any other. She is far from perfect, of course, but an excellent compromise, especially when my calculations include the thrill factor. This decision made, I turn to properly equipping her.

Most important for this trip will be good navigation gear. The charts I have bought will be of little use if I don't know where I am with some precision. For my principal navigation aid I choose a device that was a military secret a few years ago but now is widely available in the commercial market. In a short time, it has become for the mariner what the sextant once was (and for die-hard purists, remains): indispensable. The Global Positioning System unit, or GPS, is a small, relatively inexpensive, computer that uses radio signals from satellites to calculate with amazing speed and accuracy a boat's precise position. It recalculates the ever-changing position of a moving boat so quickly that it can give the speed of the boat, even a fast boat, down to tenths of a mile an hour.

Rascal is equipped with a fixed-mounted GPS unit powered by the onboard batteries. Satellite signals are received through a small, simple-looking antenna. The GPS display screen, located out of the weather in the electronics box above the helm, will tell me, among many other things: our precise position in degrees, minutes, and hundredths of minutes of latitude and longitude; our speed over the ground (which, because of the effects of currents, is often different than speed through the water); the magnetic compass heading we are on; the course on a direct line to a pre-selected destination front a point of departure; how far off the course we are and which way I should steer to get back on course; how far we have come from a point of departure; and how far it is to a given destination.

The GPS is a remarkable device, but it has two deficiencies. First, this phenomenal tool must be operated by a human being—me—thus opening up a wide range of potential disasters. Second, it is electric and thus potentially the victim of power failure. The only safeguard against the first deficiency is diligence, whose enemy, impulsiveness, is my signature trait. The potential for trouble is there, as we were later to learn the hard way. The second deficiency is more easily remedied: I buy a backup unit, hand-held, battery powered, with extra batteries, a purchase that later proves to have been prudent indeed.

Rascal is also equipped with a liquid crystal display (LCD) instrument that shows the water depth below the bottom of the hull, water temperature, speed through the water, and distance traveled since the last reset. There is a Very High Frequency—VHF—radio with weather channels, a cellular phone, a stereo radio hooked to a twelve-disk CD player with twin speakers, and an autopilot that is supposed to hold a steady course but seldom does. This was to complete the complement of *Rascal's* electronics until a friend, familiar with northern waters, said a radar was indispensable because of the fog. Reluctantly, I agree and have one installed. It's a handy, compact unit with a sixteen-mile range, but the dome, which houses the transmitter that sends out the radar beams, cannot be mounted high enough to get effectively more than about half that. That's okay though since I'll be most concerned about objects near enough to hit me or me them. A range of a mile or two is all I'll need. The more critical problem with the radar is that I get it installed only days before departure and have no idea how to operate it. I'll need to read the manual and practice along the way *before* I hit fog. And, as I am to learn, fog there will be.

In addition to the equipment that comes standard on boats like mine—electric bilge pumps, compass, navigation lights, trim tabs, gauges—I add several items. I take along the required array of safety equipment, PFDs (life jackets in conventional English, "personal flotation devices" to bureaucrats), two fire extinguishers, and a set of distress flares. I also buy another remarkable piece of technological gadgetry, a device that when switched on transmits a persistent satellite radio distress signal that allows search vessels or planes to home in on it, called an EPIRB, for Emergency Position Indicating

Radio Beacon. I add a spare set of fenders: air-filled, hard rubber, balloon-like things I will hang from the cleats and siderails of *Rascal* to protect her from scraping against hard objects, such as the concrete walls of locks. Two fifty-foot braided lines with an eye spliced into one end of both, a heavy-duty Danforth anchor, a large store of special two-cycle motor oil for the engines, a powerful, hand-held twelve-volt searchlight, a light sleeping bag, mosquito netting, fishing gear, assorted spare parts, a complete set of tools, and a hand-held bilge pump complete the list of items I'll need for the journey. I have had the boat's name and home port printed neatly on the freeboard and had her waxed top and bottom.

I set June 28 as the day of departure, later than I had wished, but I am too eager to consider postponing the adventure to next year. A few days before, I load all the gear on board and stow it, check all systems, run the motors, pick up a few small after-thoughts like extra cleaning fluids and rags and a lock for the cabin. My business affairs are in order. I have a will and have given Kitty a power of attorney to sign documents on my behalf. Butterflies are in my stomach.

I am ready to shove off.

TWO

Salt Marsh, Palms, and Pirates

St. Johns River to Chesapeake Bay

AFTER MONTHS OF PLANNING, buying charts and equipment, arranging business and personal affairs, and readying *Rascal,* the big day is finally here—and what a miserable day it is. For the past two days, a nor'easter has been blowing hard. The weather is nasty, with black clouds, fierce rain, and wind gusts to forty miles an hour. My friend, Don Lewandowski, picks me up at home at 6:30 a.m. and drives me to the Pablo Creek Marina on the Intracoastal Waterway near its intersection with the St. Johns River. In the downpour, I meet Chuck Kelly, who, operating a big forklift, removes *Rascal* gently from the dry stack and lowers her into the water. Even in the bad weather, she is beautiful. Her gelcoat glistens in the early light. In the pouring rain, I top off her fuel tanks, taking care to keep rainwater out of the filler neck, stow the last of my gear in the cabin, and fire up *Rascal's* big twin outboards. They have about 280 hours of prior use on them, barely broken in.

I cast off the lines, slip the transmissions into gear, and ease out into the ICW. Rain continues in opaque sheets. My foul-weather jacket and the T-top keep my upper body moderately dry, but my shorts and shoes are soon soaked. Gently, I ease *Rascal* up on plane and head off into the dreary weather on the start of a great adventure. Soon I realize the best thing I did in preparing for the trip was to install an

Eisinglas sheet to cover the opening between the top of the windscreen and the upper electronics box. This keeps the rain from having its way with me entirely, and, at our forty-mile-per-hour cruising speed, blinding me.

From the marina, it is only a few miles up the ICW, through a low, coastal salt marsh, to the St. Johns River. As we approach the river, I look off to port and easily see the high sand bluffs that line the south bank of the river, rising sharply from the flatness of the surrounding land. It was upon these bluffs that the French explorer René de Laudonnière in 1564 established the first French settlement in Florida, called Fort Caroline, that soon after fell to the Spanish, a pawn in the long struggle among the European powers for dominance in the New World. The Spaniard who took Ft. Caroline was Pedro Menéndez de Avilés, the man who in 1565 founded the first permanent European settlement in North America, St. Augustine, thirty miles to the south.

We cross the St. Johns diagonally in a rough chop on the beam, blown up by strong winds against an opposing current, and we pick up the ICW, continuing north. It is well known that winds blowing against opposing currents are a small boater's nightmare. I was to reaffirm this more vividly than I wished, both sooner and later on this voyage. This morning, the false dawn is overwhelmed by storm-blackened skies. Visibility in the gloom is poor as we make our way through the channel markers surrounded by miles of salt marsh dotted with tiny islands of oak and palm and pine. We pass by the salt creek that leads to Fort George Inlet, an un-navigable pass between Fort George and Talbot Island, and continue across the wide Nassau Sound and another difficult inlet, this one between Big Talbot and Amelia Islands.

Now the site of seaside homes, condos, golf courses, and upscale resorts like the Ritz-Carlton, Amelia Island was once the location of two Franciscan missions established by the early Spanish in the late sixteenth and early seventeenth centuries. North of the sound, the salt marsh narrows, squeezed between the mainland and Amelia Island. Rounding a sharp turn in the ICW, suddenly we are face to face with a giant paper mill. Its gleaming lights and belching gas against the black sky makes it look like a huge praying mantis feeding on mountains of wood chips piled at its mouth. We pass by it, then cruise slowly past the docks at the charming little town of Fernandina Beach. The town is sited at the extreme northeast corner of Florida, separated from the Georgia coastal islands by the St. Mary's River and Cumberland Sound. Fernandina Beach is the only city in America to have existed under eight flags. The inlet at this sound is deep and extremely well maintained because through it pass huge Trident nuclear submarines going to and from their base at Kings Bay, just north up the ICW.

As we head out across Cumberland Sound, we are running beam to the weather. Nasty, frothy waves slam broadside on *Rascal's* hull, sending spray high into the air and kicking her bow toward the port side. I lower the trim tabs to force her knife-like bow into the seas and I change course toward the east, heading more directly into the waves. This relieves the side pressure on the bow and smoothes the ride, but I know it's a devil's bargain. Soon enough we'll have to tack again, back to the west, to return to the ICW and our original course. Then we'll have to deal with following seas. But this turns out to be not so bad after all. As we reach the point where we must turn, we come into the lee protection of Cumberland Island. I hold the turn until we are near the island's shore, then turn sharply and run along the shoreline. The waves are smaller here, and the following seas are not as aggressive as they would have been without the lee protection. We reach the ICW again and turn north, leaving the rough sound behind.

We are still winding through a vast salt marsh, with the Kings Bay base to port and the eighteen-mile-long Cumberland Island to starboard. Past Kings Bay, we leave the ICW and take Brickhill River, which winds past Plum Orchard Mansion on Cumberland Island. There, a herd of wild horses grazes in the mansion's yard at the water's edge. The island was once a summer playground for the Carnegie family and its heirs. The mansion, and a few others on the island, is their legacy. Today, most of the island is a national park accessible only by boat.

It was the site in 1996 of the wedding of John F. Kennedy, Jr., and Carolyn Bessette.

As we leave the river, we are unaware that we are about to enter one of the most difficult passages *Rascal* will make: crossing the short but treacherous St. Andrew Inlet. Here the ICW traverses the northwest shore of Cumberland Island, then proceeds out the inlet briefly into the ocean to an outside channel marker, where it doubles back acutely toward the south end of Jekyll Island. We enter the Inlet quickly from the lee of Cumberland Island under the worst possible conditions: a strong outgoing tide and stiff onshore winds, resulting in huge, sharp-edged waves that get even bigger as they pass over shallow shoals. This morning the waves are widely spaced. I must keep *Rascal* on plane to avoid the risk of capsizing, but we can't jump from one top to the next, so we fly off the top of each, slamming into the trough between the waves, only to greet the next one frothing toward us. We pass a large motor yacht. Its captain waves. We are the only boats in sight on this black morning. *Rascal* pitches wildly in the seas. Because the charts continually fall off the console, I have to stow them. After much bone-jarring slamming, the electronics box latch shears off and the lid flails away violently. I secure it with diffi-culty, fighting to stay on my feet and keep *Rascal* on course.

Although the tide is running out, there is still high water, so I decide to cut across the shoals, shortening our route across the inlet. I turn forty-five degrees so that now the big waves are on *Rascal's* starboard beam and forequarter. The depth gauge shows only four to five feet of water here, too close for comfort, but in these conditions worth chancing. *Rascal* now, instead of slamming over head seas, is rolling into beam seas. The big waves pass over the gunwale, break-ing into the boat. With fearsome force, great sheets of green water engulf *Rascal* and me, pounding the windscreen. I begin to wonder if the bilge pumps can handle the water and whether the windscreen will shatter under the impact of these waves. Without it, I'd be com-pletely blinded. Then it is over, ending as abruptly as it began. We have reached the lee of Jekyll Island, where we pass from crashing breakers to benign inland chop. I breathe deeply and try to relax. We have survived, *Rascal* and me. It was a brief but terrifying experience, one I don't care to repeat anytime soon. Perhaps it is better that I do not know what is in store for us ahead. Back in the protection of the ICW, we cross the deep and wide St. Simons Sound, not nearly the challenge that St. Andrew Sound was, then make for the marina on St. Simons Island, where we take on fuel. There are no other fuel stops near the ICW until we reach Savannah about one hundred miles to the north.

The route from St. Simons to Savannah is remote, a vast plain of marsh grass laced through with winding creeks, narrow bays, and broad, tempestuous sounds. Here and there are tiny islands covered with old palms, pines, cedars, and oaks. The shoreline varies from black muck on which the marsh grasses grow to grayish sands along the few beaches near the inlets. We cruise along the western shore of the Georgia barrier islands, called the Golden Isles, part of the long chain of barrier islands extending from Miami to New Jersey.

No other boats are in sight. The rain has stopped, but black clouds and high winds remain. Except for St. Simons, none of these Georgia islands is accessible by car until we get to Tybee Island at the mouth of the Savannah River. The mainland side of the salt marsh is undeveloped except for the occasional tiny fishing village set deep into the marsh. Each of the islands is separated from its neighbors by a sound—a wide, deep body of water that is at once the mouth of a river, itself fed by many interconnected creeks, and an inlet from the ocean. These islands are sparsely inhabited north of St. Simons to Tybee and are as pristine as any place on the east coast of the United States. Past St. Simons, we run out the Altamaha Sound, then cut back behind Wolf Island, continue up the ICW, cross Doboy Sound, then wind through the marsh west of the spectacular Sapelo and Blackbeard Islands. The wind has decreased, though the skies are still ominous as we fly over the stiff chop in Sapelo Sound and run close alongside St. Catherines Island and across the sound of the same name. Here we run close to the beach on the south end of Ossabaw

Island, where beautiful, high white sand dunes reach out into the sound. We cross Ossabaw Sound, pass Wassaw Island, then, at last, after a long run on the twisting channel, reach the Savannah River.

Savannah is about eight miles upriver from the ICW junction. We arrive at the city in the late afternoon and tie up downtown at the dock at the Hyatt Regency Hotel. At the end of this first day, I am happily exhausted. The day has been in a small way what I hope the entire trip will be: filled with mental and physical challenge amid new landscapes and changing conditions. The ragged weather has only enhanced the day's experience.

I end this day, as I will each day hereafter, by thoroughly washing down *Rascal*, removing the corroding salt, dirt, and stains that accumulate quickly. If I fail to do this, *Rascal's* finish will deteriorate rapidly. I refill her oil tanks, top off with fuel, and replace the sheared electronics box latch with a spare I brought along. All this work, after a demanding day at the helm, leaves me completely drained, but elated. The feeling is one I never achieved from a hard day at the office. It is both physical and mental exhaustion combined with a sense of having mastered adversity to accomplish my objective.

Savannah occupies a high, oak-covered bluff over the river, about sixteen miles upstream from the sea. The Hyatt is built on the site where in 1733 James Oglethorpe and his band of 114 colonists pitched their tents on their first day in the New World, founding the last of the original thirteen colonies. Now huge cargo ships ply the river a rock's throw from where we are docked.

James Edward Oglethorpe was a dedicated utopian and successful militarist, a man filled with compassion for the less fortunate of his time, unless he happened to be killing them in battle. So motivated, he and a band of like-minded people assembled a party of England's outcasts: imprisoned debtors, poor farmers and shopkeepers, and oppressed religious minorities. They arrived on the future site of the Hyatt Regency, filled with dreams for the future, determined to establish a permanent settlement in which Oglethorpe's vision of personal conduct and social justice would create the near-perfect life.

Believing that he knew best how others should conduct their lives, a hallmark of Utopians and collectivists everywhere, Oglethorpe forbade "distilled liquors," lawyers, and slavery. He had commendable objectives, perhaps, but he failed to account for what can loosely be called human nature. Booze has been favored by mankind since people learned how to make the stuff, particularly, as here, by people living in harsh conditions. Oglethorpe's group figured out they could buy it from nearby tradesmen, and they did. Lawyers nearly overran the place because Oglethorpe, in his cocoon of idealism, had failed to set up even a basic means for settling disputes. Slavery flourished mainly because it was so profitable.

Oglethorpe acquitted himself better on the battlefield. He seems not to have been troubled by the dichotomy that he was compassionate, philanthropical utopian, and extremely effective at killing people. He moved his headquarters to Fort Frederica on St. Simons Island, which *Rascal* and I passed on the ICW just before making our turn up the Savannah River. From there he taunted the Spanish by claiming for England all the lands south to the St. Johns River. When the War of Jenkins's Ear between England and Spain was declared, Oglethorpe attacked the Spanish at St. Augustine. He easily captured the town and its surrounding outposts but was unable to conquer the impregnable Castillo de San Marcos. He returned to Georgia empty handed. He got even with the Spanish when a large force of them attacked him on St. Simons Island and were soundly defeated in the Battle of Bloody Marsh, memorialized today by a small monument at the site. Shortly after the battle, Oglethorpe, his utopian dreams shattered, returned to England, never to visit the New World again.

~~~

I cast off the lines and head for Charleston. The route is lovely on a picture-perfect day. We pass Daufuskie Island, cross Calibogue Sound, and arrive at Hilton Head Island. We take a turn around Harbor Town's attractive Euro-style harbor. Leaving Hilton Head, we cross Port Royal Sound and head toward Beaufort (pronounced "bew-firt"), South

Carolina. The area is magnificent: pristine salt marsh, oak hammocks, white beaches, and tiny, isolated islands.

Passing Beaufort, the ICW winds through the deep rivers and elegant marshes of South Carolina's Low Country. The dominant ethos of South Carolina has been called the Warrior Culture by one author and the Cracker Culture by another. It could as well be called the Celtic Culture. It is the culture of the Deep South, people whose antecedents came from the lowlands of Scotland, the north of Ireland, and the northern counties of England and migrated to America primarily from 1718 to 1775. They brought their ancient Celtic culture with them, a culture that thrives today, in a milder form, and explains much of the difference between the people of the North and those of the South. The term "Cracker" originally meant one who "talked boastingly." Other descriptions of these early immigrants to the South were even less complimentary. As Professor McWhiney writes in *Cracker Culture*,

> *"Throughout the antebellum period a wide range of observers generally characterized Southerners as more hospitable, generous, frank, courteous, spontaneous, lazy, lawless, militaristic, wasteful, impractical, and reckless than Northerners, who were in turn more reserved, shrewd, disciplined, gauche, enterprising, acquisitive, careful, frugal, ambitious, pacific, and practical than Southerners. The Old South was a leisure-oriented society that fostered idleness and gaiety, where people favored the spoken word over the written and enjoyed their sensual pleasures. Family ties reportedly were stronger in the South than in the North; Southerners, whose values were more agrarian than those of Northerners, wasted more time and consumed more tobacco and liquor and were less concerned with the useful and the material." (p. 268)*

The one characteristic that describes Southerners' greatest difference from the Puritan culture of the North is the importance they placed on leisure and their indifference toward, if not outright antipathy for, work. Like their Celtic ancestors, they loved to hunt, fish, gamble, drink to excess, tell stories, dance, and whore around— in short, do anything but productive labor, which they left to their wives or, if they could afford them, their slaves. More commonly, the work was simply left undone. Some of that folkway persists today. If a complex cultural phenomenon can be reduced to a bumper sticker, I saw it on the rusted-out bumper of a broken-down pickup truck parked in front of a honky-tonk in South Carolina: "Jesus is coming. Look like you're working." No less an authority than the revered General Robert E. Lee remarked, "Our people are opposed to work.... Our troops, officers, community, and press. All ridicule and resist it."

The Warrior Culture has one other important characteristic that immigrants to the South brought with them from their ancient home-lands and have consistently shown ever since: They resolutely resist authority in any form, but especially from government. Since the debates surrounding the adoption of the U.S. Constitution and the Bill of Rights, through events preceding the War Between the States, and continuing through its consistently conservative voting patterns, the Deep South has remained vigorously opposed to a strong, activist central government. This, as we will see when we arrive in New England, contrasts sharply with the Puritan communal ideals.

Entering Charleston Harbor from the ICW is an exciting moment. There, suddenly before us, is the Battery and this jewel of a town. Founded in 1670, periodically pillaged and burned, rebuilt, again and again, its economy wrecked and reborn, the city today is an exquisitely restored, romantic place unlike any other city in America. Its architectural theme is eighteenth- and nineteenth-century British colonial with strong influence from the Caribbean. Its history, however, will always be dominated by April 12, 1861. It was then that Edmund Ruffin, a sixty-seven-year-old farm paper editor, pulled the lanyard on a cannon mounted at Fort Johnson, opening fire on Fort Sumter and starting the War Between the States. The South's artillery was commanded by General P. G. T. Beauregard, the North's by his former artillery instructor at West Point, Major Robert Anderson.

Thirty-four hours later Anderson surrendered the badly battered Fort Sumter without casualties, and the rest is long, dark history.

I end the day by washing *Rascal* down after we have tied up at the Charleston City Marina, site of the start and finish of the last two Around Alone sailboat races, truly epic undertakings in which both men and women skipper amazing sailing machines 27,000 miles around the world, alone.

~~~

In the early morning, I can tell this will be a fine day. It is warm and sunny and the winds are calm. We cruise slowly along the north bank of the Ashley River, round the famed Battery, and drift slowly along the shore of Charleston's downtown area. I look again at the charts and decide to take a break from the narrow confines of the ICW and run the next leg in the ocean, offshore. We head out toward the mouth of the harbor in the South Channel, passing old Castle Pinckney on Shutes Folly Island and Fort Johnson, and approach Fort Sumter. It sits on a tiny plot of land, with deep water of the channel on one side and not much depth at all on the other. Straight across the channel about a mile away, perched ominously on the beach, is Fort Moultrie, site of one of the first Patriot victories in the Revolutionary War.

I ease *Rascal* up on plane and out of the harbor into the open ocean, turning north a couple of miles offshore. The water is murky and shallow. Just ahead, stretching for miles across our intended path, between us and deeper water, is a line of frothy white breakers. In my eagerness to run in the ocean, I assumed—mistakenly— there would be deep water this far offshore. I am not equipped with coastal charts; I am flying blind in what I can now see is a vast patchwork of shoals extending for miles along the coast and out to sea. Because shrimp boats are working beyond the breakers, I know they must be in deeper water. The tide is almost high. I figure that if the water under these low breakers is deep enough, we can simply power through them and get farther out to sea where the shrimpers are working. We come off plane and slowly approach one of the bars where the waves are breaking. The depth gauge reads three feet. We head bow first straight into a breaker, and the depth holds. Now I know the waves are breaking at three feet, a depth we can easily pass over on plane. I get *Rascal* on plane again and plow headlong into first one, then another line of breakers as we head out toward deeper water. At last, we break free into open water and once again turn north up the coast, cruising about five miles offshore.

It is late afternoon now, and the wind picks up. With it, the waves grow quickly over the shallow bottom. I lower the trim tabs and change course to attack the waves more on the bow. Up ahead a few miles, I can now see the long jetties that extend out from shore to form the entrance channel into Winyah Bay, our destination. We make for the seaward end of the jetties and, as we reach the end, turn west between them. They are several hundred yards apart and newly built of piled-up rock. It will be a rough ride for the three miles or so of their length from the shore. The tide is running out strongly, and the now freshened wind is blowing against it. The waves between the jetties become huge, and while they are mostly on the bow, big, erratic cross-waves bounce off both confining jetty walls and slam into *Rascal* from both sides. The sea, caught in this man-made rip rap corridor, is churning confusion. *Rascal* pitches about wildly, her hull flies out of the water, and her big motors, with no water to resist the props, scream as the RPMs jump. I quickly pull back on the throttles to keep from blowing the motors, then open them when she lands again. She hits hard, sending a shudder through her fiberglass hull. I am drenched by the walls of spray kicked up as *Rascal* charges toward shore. The windshield, with no wipers, offers zero visibility, and since I have to stand out from behind it to see, I get blasted full in the face by torrents of seawater. I can see just enough to stay off the rocks and enough to avoid the few other boats caught in this maelstrom.

At last, we break through the last of the rough water and enter the blessedly calm waters of Winyah Bay. Up the wide, flat calm bay we cruise, spoil islands lining the channel, shallow water everywhere outside the channel. This bay is the confluence of the Waccamaw and Great Pee Dee Rivers, which join at historic Georgetown. Here we refuel and, on a beautiful afternoon, cruise up the Waccamaw. Its banks are covered in dense, primitive forest. There are no signs of man on its shores. The river, however, is another matter. It is Sunday and the river is clogged with hundreds of craft of every imaginable description—inner tubes, pontoon paddle boats, bowriders, dilapidated houseboats, ancient wooden cabin cruisers, ski boats pulling wild-eyed teens, john boats with annoyed fishermen, powerful high-performance race boats, sparkling new family cruisers, and pesky jet skis buzzing like mosquitoes. Even above the drone of *Rascal's* motors, the noise is a cacophony. Deafening roars from the hot-rod boats, irritating high-pitched whines from the jet skis, and shrill screams of delight from teenaged girls fill the air. In the midst of it all, we cruise warily along. I keep a close eye on the traffic but enjoy this wild, chaotic scene. As the river winds its way through the magnificent forests, it gets progressively narrower and the traffic denser. It is now becoming dangerous, and the water surface is a jumble of intermixed wakes colliding into each other, nearly swamping the smaller boats.

Then, as we round a bend in the river, suddenly the ICW enters a ditch and the Waccamaw River turns off to port. Soon I realize where all the activity has come from. We have reached the tourist mecca of Myrtle Beach. The high banks of the ICW here are not pretty. Pontoon boat and jet ski rental places explain part of the traffic. There are water slides, goofy golf courses, T-shirt shops, fast food outlets, gas stations, convenience stores, trailer parks ("manufactured housing communities," in current euphemese), motels of every size and shape, restaurants of every description, and on and on. Rampant commercial chaos. Unrestrained self-expression. This is a playground for the Warrior Culture.

Gratefully, we depart Myrtle Beach and cruise the short distance to the border between South and North Carolina. Just over the state line, we pass the small community of Calabash, seafood restaurant capitol of the Carolinas, then continue along a long, uneventful stretch of the ICW. The waterway runs in a generally east-west direction along this stretch of the North Carolina coast. The land pushes out into the sea and ends in the state's infamous shoals and the capes that mark them, Cape Fear, Cape Lookout, Cape Hatteras. Along this leg, the ocean is just a mile or so to the south of the ICW. We pass through small fishing villages and towns clogged with vacation homes, condos, and commercial sprawl. There are hundreds of boats and numerous marinas and seafood restaurants and bars in the larger towns. Rustic quaintness abounds in the smaller villages. Low coastal woods with oaks draped in Spanish moss, coastal pines, and a few palms and salt marsh line the waterway.

At last, after a long day, we stop for the night at the charming fishing village of Southport, at the mouth of the Cape Fear River, just inside the inlet of the same name. The town is sparkling clean, its style reminiscent of the antebellum South. Along the low waterfront are modest wood clapboard homes freshly painted white with black shutters, their yards ragged in the sandy soil. Some date back to the mid-1800s. At one corner of the waterfront is a collection of ramshackle seafood restaurants raised off grade on wood pilings. I soon see why. As the tide comes in and begins to reach its peak, amplified by the full moon, seawater flows up to the restaurants, then over the parking lots and streets in front of them. Makeshift walkways are set up to keep the patrons' feet dry.

Up the Cape Fear River is the historic town of Wilmington. Along with Charleston, it was one of the last ports used by Confederate blockade runners in the Civil War, the others stoppered by the Union Navy as part of the Anaconda Plan to strangle the South. Just offshore from Southport, extending thirty miles out to sea, is the notorious Frying Pan Shoals, an underwater graveyard for countless ships and their passengers and crew. These have contributed over many years to the fearsome reputation of the Outer Banks of North Carolina.

~~~

Rascal is not happy. Since yesterday she acts as if her motors are running on only eleven of their twelve cylinders. They are sluggish and her starboard motor needs extra throttle to hold its RPM. We stop in Wrightsville Beach at a large marina, where I convince the marina manager to have his busy mechanic at least diagnose the problem. After a lot of high-tech talk, he decides we need a new stator, a main component of the ignition system, which the marina does not have. I call another marina up the ICW and they have it. As we are about to leave, a loud, slightly drunk voice blares out over the VHF for all to hear. With an uneasy grasp of standard radio procedure, Booger Man calls the Coast Guard: "Uh, U.S. Coast Guard, this here's the Booger Man. We got a body floating in the water."

Her voice carrying a hint of incredulousness, the radio operator says, "U.S. Coast Guard, Wrightsville Beach, responding to the last calling vessel."

Using CB radio vernacular, "You got the Booger Man, come on back."

"U.S. Coast Guard, Wrightsville Beach, what kind of body?"

Not given to prolixity, he responds, "A person."

"U.S. Coast Guard, Wrightsville Beach, is it alive?" Buried somewhere in a Coast Guard radio operators manual is an instruction that every transmission is to be preceded by an identification tag, a needlessly cumbersome formality the operator includes throughout the exchange, but I will omit from here on.

> BM: "It's dead."
> CG: "Have you tried to tell if it's alive?"
> BM: "No, it's floating face down and it's all white. Looks like the crabs have been after it. It's dead."
> CG: "Is it male or female?"
> BM: "It's an old man."
> CG: "Is it dressed?"
> BM "Yes."
> CG: "What kind of clothes does it have on?"
> BM: "Plaid shirt and gray pants."
> CG: "Where are you located?"
> BM: "In the middle of the waterway just south of you."

> CG: "Can you stand by until a boat arrives?"
> BM: In a reluctant tone of voice, as though the beer supply
> has run low and needs replenishing, "Well, I guess so."

Everyone listening to their VHF on that hot, sultry day has a good laugh at Booger Man's antics and the Coast Guard's response. It turns out some very old gentleman apparently had a heart attack and fell off a dock.

I pick up the part and head on to Beaufort (pronounced "bow-fort"), North Carolina, passing through a brief squall on the way. Beaufort is a picturesque nautical town, founded in 1709, today nicely restored, with marine facilities lining its shores. It sits just inside the Beaufort Inlet on a peninsula jutting out from the mainland at the south end of the Outer Banks. Its sister town, Morehead City, is not much more than a few miles across the Newport River. Convention seems to have it that the Outer Banks begin at Cape Fear Inlet near Southport. One look at the charts, though, and I am convinced they begin here, at Shackleford Banks, just across the water from Beaufort. Here begins the long, pencil-thin, lazy reverse C that defines the Banks. I am so intrigued by the geography and the chance to cruise the famous Pamlico and Albemarle Sounds that I decide again to forsake the ICW and strike out on my own. The narrow confines of the ditch have grown wearying; I'm ready for more interesting waters.

~~~

On a warm, sunny morning, we leave the Beaufort docks and head out over the pale green waters into Core Sound. Lying between the mainland and the Core Banks, the sound is a wide, shallow body of water with marsh grasses lining its shores. It is so shallow— channel depths are three to six feet and outside the channel, one to two feet—that larger boats never come this way. The channel is marked, but the markers are far apart, each out of sight of the next. I don't have adequate charts. Mine cover the ICW well, but for this area, the scale does not provide enough detail. Using binoculars, I try to spot the next marker, with mixed success. The water is too murky, stirred up by recent winds, to judge the depth by color variation. I decide just to keep a close eye on the depth gauge, avoid areas where I see birds wading or marsh grass protruding, and wing it. The day is glorious, the water has only a light chop, and *Rascal* is flying happily along. We pass the fishing village of Atlantic and just beyond it turn hard west across a small bay, into a tiny waterway enclosed by wide fields of marsh grass and swamp. Great blue herons, flocks of ibis and egrets, lone cormorants, and anhingas are all around. The roar of *Rascal's* motors scares a few into flight, but most just stare warily. We pass into another small bay, through an old canal, and finally, regrettably, leave this serene, coastal wilderness and make our way into the wide, deep Neuse River.

I feel elation. Flying across the water at more than forty miles an hour, with the sun gently warming me and welcome breezes wafting around the windscreen, I am as close to heaven as it is possible to get, here on this day. On the open water I am, in my mind at least, in a state of nearly perfect freedom. There are none of the annoying little rules claimed to be necessary for modern life in a dense population. There are no traffic signals, no designated driving lanes, and no speed limits. There are no cops. I do not have to wear a helmet or a seat belt. Although they are making inroads, the nagging nannies, always so eager to protect me from myself, have not yet overrun my little slice of freedom. I will treasure it while I can.

We head across the Neuse River to Oriental, North Carolina, for a quick visit. It's a tiny village (pop. 850) but home to more than fifteen hundred sailboats. The dockmaster where I refuel moved here from Kansas seven years ago just to sail. He had sailed for years on reservoirs in the Midwest and had dreamed of sailing inside the Outer Banks, which is, he says, the finest sailing ground in America. He retired in his fifties, moved here, took this part-time job, and lives on his twenty-nine-foot boat. His dream is now a reality, and he is a contented man.

We head out the Neuse and across the Pamlico Sound in a nasty chop, trim tabs almost fully extended. I finally locate the Dog Slough

Channel leading through ugly shoals into the village at Ocracoke, one of the most remote places on the east coast of the U.S. The simplest way to get here is by ferry from the mainland, or you can drive forever down nearly the whole length of the Outer Banks, the islands in many places not much wider than the road, using bridges and short ferries to cross the inlets. It is not a place you happen upon; you have to want to come here. For this reason, it is one of the last outposts of Americans speaking naturally with an English accent. The older residents here still have the accents of Devon or Cornwall in England's West Country, whence came their ancestors a few centuries ago. 'High tide" is pronounced "hoi toid."

Ocracoke (sometimes Okracoke) is a fine, well-protected harbor right alongside an inlet of the same name through the Outer Banks. The inlet and the waters around the entry channels into the harbor are among the most treacherous anywhere, waiting to ensnare any boat that ventures this way without local knowledge, good charts, or a pilot. It was these dubious attractions that made the place a desirable lair for Edward Teach, better known as Blackbeard, one of the bloodiest pirates ever to sail the seas. And it was here at Ocracoke on November 22, 1718, that Blackbeard's ship *Adventure* was attacked by two sloops, *Ranger* and *Jane,* under the command of Lieutenant Robert Maynard of the British Navy. Both Navy vessels promptly ran aground on the surrounding sandbars, but with help from the rising tide, floated free and moved to the attack once again. The *Ranger* took a devastating broadside from *Adventure* and fell off, but Maynard in the *Jane* got close enough to *Adventure* to be boarded by the pirates. In a scene that might have come from a Hollywood movie, Maynard and crew engaged the hideous, violent Blackbeard and his smaller band of pirates in a cutlass and pistol duel. Cut twenty times and hit by five shots, Blackbeard was at last killed by the swipe of a broadsword that cut off his head. Maynard had the gruesome trophy hung from the bowsprit of his sloop.

~~~

Early in the morning, we leave the lovely harbor at Ocracoke, ease out of Dog Slough Channel and into Pamlico Sound. The calm waters and clouded skies of the harbor do not hint that the sound is windswept and choppy. But *Rascal* is up to the task. I set a course of about sixty degrees as we head up the sound toward Roanoke Island. Speeding along just out of the harbor, I fail to notice in the gray light of morning a seine net strung between two fish weirs. *Rascal* merely blinks as she slices through the top lines of this unmarked obstruction and continues on her way. These weirs, or traps, require constant vigilance while a boat is running close to shore. The wind, and hence the seas, are from the south- southeast, and thus mostly on the stern. I trim *Rascal,* making gentle adjustments until she is riding as smoothly as the seas will allow. No fast boat rides well in a following sea, but *Rascal* is as happy as she can get in these conditions.

We pass the town of Hatteras on our starboard, the profile of her stately lighthouse outlined against the early morning sky, and find calmer water over the shoals. I decide to enter the Manteo Channel at its western end rather than cut it short because the chart shows large spoil areas, some dry. The large island looming up before us, just inside the Outer Banks, is the place where, on July 13, 1584, English explorers arrived on two ships chartered by Sir Walter Raleigh. They were taken by the exotic beauty of the place, largely unchanged to this day. They befriended the Algonquin Indians and returned to England with two, named Manteo and Wanchese. Raleigh chartered a second expedition of settlers. Once arrived, this group promptly got at odds with the Indians and had to be rescued by Sir Francis Drake. Undeterred, the persistent Raleigh organized a third effort that was based on Roanoke Island. It was led by Governor White, whose daughter, Eleanor, married to Ananias Dare, gave birth to the first child of English parents born in the New World, Virginia Dare. This effort too was beset with Indian problems, forcing White to return to England for help. After many long delays and crises, White returned two and a half years later to find . . . nothing. All the houses and all the people formerly in them had just disappeared; only a palisade remained.

White found the word "Croatan" carved in a tree, but nobody to this day knows what became of the colonists. Today, the two principal towns on this historic island are Manteo on the north end and Wanchese on the south, named for the two Algonquin Indians taken to England. It still is a spectacularly beautiful place, sitting inside the Outer Banks between Roanoke and Croatan Sounds to the east and west and between Pamlico Sound to the south and Albemarle Sound to the north.

We enter Albemarle Sound just as the wind kicks up still more and the seas become a mess. There is a choice of direction to be made. We can leave the Albemarle Sound by heading up the Pasquotank River to Elizabeth City, where the river narrows, then winds north to join the Great Dismal Swamp Canal. The canal, dug in colonial times, is a long, dull stretch through the Dismal Swamp, aptly named, that ends near Norfolk. Recent heavy rains have flooded the swamp, and as a result, the canal is littered with floating logs. These, if we should hit them, could damage the props or, worse, tear the lower ends off the motors. If that should happen deep in the swamp, we'd be in a fix. The alternative route, which I decide we'll take, follows the North River through Coinjock Bay, North Landing River, and into the Albemarle and Chesapeake Canal to Norfolk. We slog along with the weather on the port quarter until at last, we reach the calm waters of the North River, where we rejoin the ICW and make for Norfolk. At Great Bridge, just south of Norfolk, is a lock. Except for a lock in the Dismal Swamp route, it is the only lock on the eastern ICW. Here, I talk with a couple in a fifty-foot sailboat, who are nearing the end of a five-year around-the-world odyssey. They plan to sell their boat when they get home and not buy another. Their adventure then will be behind them. In our brief talk, I sense they are relieved to have completed their voyage, will treasure the experience for a lifetime, but are finished with boats for a long while, maybe forever. In fact, if I have read them correctly, they may be finished with each other too. The mills of the gods grind slow, but in boats especially, they grind exceedingly fine.

As the ICW enters the Elizabeth River at Norfolk, a stunning panorama opens before us. There, in their hulking splendor, are dozens of the U.S. Navy ships-of-line: an awkward-looking but lethal flat-top, guided-missile frigates, sleek destroyers, and submarines. There are also mammoth supply ships, minesweepers, harbor tugs, and more. We are in the midst of the Norfolk Naval Shipyard, a gigantic marina for Navy ships in repair. What a sight! We pass closely among them, dwarfed by these massive steel giants. Dead ahead is Norfolk's Waterside development with a modern marina, riverwalk, shopping center, huge marine exhibit, hotels, office buildings. We dock right alongside the riverwalk. A passing shower strands me in *Rascal's* cabin. Enclosed in darkness for a few minutes in a quiet cave with only the sound of the pouring rain outside, I lapse into a peaceful nap at the end of a tiring but wonderful day of adventures. Tomorrow promises still more.

THREE

Annapolis on the Fourth
Chesapeake Bay to New York City

BY NOW I HAVE REGAINED MY SEAMANSHIP SKILLS. For the first few days, I was critical of the many lapses I showed—shaky docking skills, errant navigation, uncertain boat trim, forgotten routines, and more. Even at seemingly simple things, such as securing the boat to a dock, or refilling oil tanks, I am error prone. But now the skills return. Mistakes are corrected, routines learned. I gain the confidence I will surely need in the weeks that lie ahead.

The day dawns gloriously. It is a cloudless blue sky, with gentle winds. The temperature is very cool, maybe sixty degrees—in early July! As *Rascal* breaks the glassy smooth waters of the Elizabeth River and surges ahead, I think about how historic these waters are. We soon are crossing Hampton Roads, fought over many times as the key to control of the Chesapeake and the site of the epic, if inconclusive, battle between the *USS Monitor* and the *CSS Virginia* (formerly the *USS MerrimacV*). We pass Fortress Monroe on Old Point Comfort, lying at the end of the history-laden peninsula formed by the York and the James Rivers. Here is where General George McClelland's abortive peninsula campaign began and ended.

Hampton Roads is the confluence of the Elizabeth River coming up from the south through Norfolk, the James River flowing in from the northwest, and the Chesapeake Bay to the northeast. Just up the

James, where the river narrows, three ships—the *Susan Constant, Discovery,* and *Godspeed*—arrived from England in 1607 and dropped anchor. A small band of settlers from these ships built a tiny toehold of English civilization there called Jamestown, headed by John Smith. The attempt at permanence finally succumbed to the usual problems of early settlements: plague, crop failure, dissension, and, always, the Indians.

Across the peninsula from Jamestown, on the York River, is Yorktown. Here in 1781 a combined land force of French soldiers under the Comte de Rochambeau, Patriots under Washington, and contingents under Anthony Wayne and the Marquis de Lafayette, supported by a French fleet under Admiral de Grasse, defeated the British under Lord Cornwallis. When Cornwallis surrendered his sword to General George Washington, a new nation was born. Yorktown was also where, eighty-one years later, Confederate soldiers under General Joseph E. Johnston anchored their left flank in a defensive line across the peninsula, a line that confused and delayed General George McClelland's Union forces. The Confederates occupied the same trenches and field fortifications that Cornwallis's men had constructed.

As we leave the lee protection of Hampton Roads's shores and head into Chesapeake Bay, we get an unpleasant surprise. The winds now are blowing hard and steady, straight out of the north, coming at us. There are small craft warnings. Wind speed is thirty to thirty-five miles an hour. We try to gain some protection by hugging the west shore, but in doing so we get off track and wind up in Mobjack Bay. We have to backtrack to get back in the Chesapeake. While backtracking, we find a short stretch of quiet water and, absentmindedly, I watch commercial fishermen in a skiff pulling in a seine net. Too late I realize the net is unmarked and must lie across our intended path. Quickly, I cut the throttles back, and *Rascal* drops off plane. Now I see the small floats of the net and sense the fishermen are watching closely. I slam the transmissions into reverse and apply power just in time. The net passes under *Rascal's* hull to about midship but no farther. The net is saved from damage by the powerful props. I wave to the fishermen, who don't bother to acknowledge but go back to their labors.

Once we are back on course in the bay, the seas are now running four to five feet, very steep with wide intervals, making it impossible to prevent the hull from pounding. *Rascal* flies off the top of one wave, then crashes into the trough only to fly over the top of the next. When she lands in the trough at thirty-five miles an hour, it is with a bone-jarring violence that I worry may cause something to break. This goes on hour after hour, testing my will to press on. The violence in the boat makes it impossible to read the face of the GPS to tell what course we are on, but the large numbers on the compass tell me we are headed due north.

Just as I think it can't possibly get any worse—it does. The mouth of the Potomac under these conditions is among the most treacherous waters anywhere, and that is just where we are. Seas are now running six feet or so and incredibly steep, forced upward by the outgoing river current running into the incoming tide over a comparatively shallow bottom, this is in thirty-mile-per-hour winds. I look around and notice there are no other boats nearby. The few sailboats I see in the distance are wisely avoiding this area, and all have two or three reefs in their mainsails, or no main at all, and a storm jib. It's too late, however; we are now caught in the middle of this mayhem. *Rascal* is flying so badly that her entire hull, motors and all, leaves the water as the props spin wildly in thin air. I am being tossed around in the cockpit, drenched continually by massive sheets of spray kicked up when *Rascal* crashes through the heavy seas. I have the trim tabs locked all the way down, trying to force the light bow down so it will not fly too badly but fly it does. I try bringing her off plane, slowed to a crawl, but that only makes things worse. Without power, her bow is at the mercy of the waves and stands almost straight up with each passing wave, then crashes violently into the trough behind. I bring her back up on plane and try something desperate: to apply more downward force on the bow, I speed up, opening the throttles to nearly full speed. It works. The motors are screaming at 4500 RPM, and the boat is now a waterborne rocket careening through the seas. The added downforce presses *Rascal's* bow hard into the oncoming waves, slicing through them rather than getting kicked over them. A sense of relief comes over me, mixed with satisfaction that I have prevailed over these threatening conditions, found the tenacity to press ahead, and solved this ugly problem not by backing off but by throttling up. I also wonder why I didn't think of the solution sooner. Another lesson learned.

At last, we have crossed the mouth of the Potomac and head for the village of Solomons for lunch and fuel, then on to Annapolis. Here in the upper bay, the high winds have less effect on the water. The waves are far less troublesome. I ease up on the trim tabs and feel *Rascal* surge forward, released from the restraining drag of the tabs. I apply more throttle, trying to keep down pressure on the bow. We are running at nearly fifty miles an hour.

Approaching Annapolis, I see hundreds of sailboats of every description, sails filled and heeled over in the stiff wind. Some are running with the wind, others on port or starboard tack. Apparent chaos abounds. How they avoid a collision I can't imagine. The scene reminds me of the bumper car ride at the county fair. I am vigilant in order not to hit anybody, and we take the channel into the harbor at slow speed. As we enter the harbor, I am struck by the beauty of the place. The Naval Academy is off to starboard, sitting on a neck between the harbor and the Severn River. Its massive Greek Revival architecture is elegant. Towering over it is the huge copper dome of the Navy chapel, splendid in its verdigris patina. All around the harbor are handsome low-rise condos, marinas filled with fine boats, restaurants, the Marriott Hotel where I will stay, and more. It is surely among the loveliest harbors I've ever seen. At the west end of the harbor is a small draw span that we get under easily, entering into an idyllic creek lined with beautiful homes, each with its own dock and boats. The smell of fresh-cut grass is in the air, and huge spruce trees line the banks. The creek is wide enough that there are twenty or so sailboats anchored in midchannel. I cruise to the end of the creek, astounded at the quiet beauty of this place and think this is where I might want to live someday, right here on this creek. Later, I am told there are more such creeks around Annapolis, and all are equally attractive.

We return to the harbor and dock at the hotel, with a bar and restaurant right at our slip. Outdoor tables line the dock area. It is a perfect spot. This is the Fourth of July and tonight the city will have fireworks shot from a huge barge at the center of the harbor. A traditional holiday parade goes by with bands, fire engines, and all the rest. The streets are jammed, and the crowd's festive. The weather is perfect, maybe seventy degrees, low humidity, and a mild breeze. My spirits are high as I reflect on how fortunate I am to be able to see this charming place on such a day. Life is good!

Rascal's slip sits at the entrance to a dead-end canal that's maybe 150 yards long and lined with boats tied parallel to the bulkhead. The canal is only about thirty yards wide and now is the site of an impromptu parade of boats of every description. They cruise up and down this grand, nautical boulevard, seeing and being seen, and I have the best seat in the house. There are tiny dinghies powered by tiny outboards, some even rowed; magnificent sailboats; family motor cruisers; noisy high-performance boats; glistening restored antique runabouts; a miniature tugboat. On schedule, the fireworks light up the sky over the harbor to conclude a truly magnificent day filled with emotions and savored with all the senses. I wish it would not end.

~~~

The next morning, I tend to repairs. The latches that secure the two deck hatches have cracked badly from the pounding *Rascal* has taken, so I buy replacement parts and will install them later. Finally, it is time to say goodbye to Annapolis and head across and down the bay to St. Michaels, Maryland, only about thirty miles away. The day is glorious, not a cloud anywhere, low humidity, and maybe seventy-five degrees. My heart is reluctant to leave as we head out of this beautiful place. Once out of the slow-speed zone, I advance the throttles, and *Rascal* leaps ahead. We are both eager. The RPMs jump to three thousand.

The motors strain to get *Rascal* out of the confining grip of the sea and onto the top of the waves. After a few seconds, she breaks free, as the powerful thrust of the big twin motors pushes her out of the hole. I know we are on top when the RPMs leap up to 4200 with no more throttle advance. The props scream as the boat's hull breaks on top. I retard throttle to four thousand RPM, a comfortable cruising speed at roughly forty-three miles an hour. The seas are magnificent, just bumpy enough to tease *Rascal* but not require much effort. She runs free. We are flying, and sailboats flash by like fence posts. We round a point, making for St. Michaels. The sailboats, all of them, are fearful of the shoals that extend out from the point and they steer wide. *Rascal* draws just over knee deep on a plane, not the five feet and more of most sailboats. We cut the shoals short, throwing caution to the wind, dodging the omnipresent crab pots. The depth gauge flashes its shallow water warning, but we blast ahead and clear the shoals safely. Success. We head on for our destination, glorying in every mile, passing every boat in sight.

At this time of year, St. Michaels is dedicated to tourism. It is not yet a Disney sort of place but headed there. My hotel is a charming, if overly popular, spot with its own docks. I persuade the female dock-master (dockmistress?) to let us raft up to a local boat. After securing *Rascal*, I set about installing the new deck latches, and it turns out to be a chore. The new latches, though they come from a well-known U.S. manufacturer, are badly designed. They are not nearly as well-made or cleverly designed as the parts they replace. The original parts should be made of stainless steel rather than plastic, but otherwise, they are perfect. After some frustration in the heat of the afternoon, the task is complete.

I walk around the harbor to the one place that makes St. Michaels worth the visit: the Chesapeake Bay Maritime Museum and its fine collection of restored old working boats from the area. Among many others, there is a sloop-rigged work boat the locals call a skipjack. This, I recall my Grandfather Thomas telling me, was the kind of boat he and his father and brothers worked on as oystermen in the bay.

The old oyster rakes they used in his day are on display. He grew up on St. George Island in the Potomac River, just upstream from the bay. He was the first member of his large family to leave the island in search of a better life. Oystering then was extremely hard, dangerous work, and not all that profitable. He never regretted leaving and lived to be a hundred years old. I think he made the right move.

~~~

Again, today's travels will be fairly short, only about seventy miles. We get a late start in perfect weather, have a nice run under the monstrous bridge that stretches high over the bay at Annapolis, and continue up the bay to the Sassafras River. There, about five miles upriver, sits the Kitty Knight House Inn on a high bluff above the river, with a commanding view. Conveniently, at the foot of the bluff is a fine marina. I get a slip under cover, close to the inn. The popular inn seems a little tired and moderately frazzled, understandable, perhaps for a place built in the mid-1700s. The inn has a verandah and gazebo bar with a spectacular view down the Sassafras River. The sun sets over the low, tree-covered hills that line the river's banks, and I think what a truly beautiful place this is.

~~~

We get away early for the two-hundred-mile leg that will take us to see my old friend Jack McCormick, in Bay Head, New Jersey, and promptly encounter fog. This is our first encounter with the stuff, and I am thankful it is not too thick. Visibility is maybe half a mile. Fortunately, I have practiced using the radar along the way and, at least, know how to get it going, though my skills at reading the display are undeveloped. With its help, I find the entrance to the creek at the top of the bay, leading to the Chesapeake and Delaware Canal, and do it without slowing from our usual cruising speed of about forty miles per hour. The radar will warn me of fixed objects ahead and show me the outlines of the coast. It will even show other boats, though with less dependability. Fiberglass does not reflect radar beams well and therefore unless a boat has a fairly large motor or some other sub-stantial steel object, it will be nearly invisible to the radar. Sailboats usually, but not always, carry a radar reflector, but even these are not always reliable. In short, the radar display, particularly one interpreted by a novice operator, is not foolproof in warning of other boats. It's helpful as a tool to aid vigilance.

The C&D Canal is empty of other boats on this calm, foggy Sunday morning. I pass through its fifteen miles without incident, enter the wide Delaware River and swing east. Happily, the fog has lifted, the sky is clear and the river is table flat for most of the fifty-mile run to the ocean. Only near Cape May, New Jersey, does the river hint at its fearsome reputation among sailors. A moderate chop kicks up, then a heavy fog sets in out of nowhere. One minute we are flying along under blue sky, the next idling in a thick cloud with visibility of twenty yards. Again, the radar helps, showing small boats anchored all around us, their occupants fishing in the eerie pale light cast by this morning fog. We find the entrance to the Cape May Canal and through a gap in the fog see many boats leaving the canal, headed out into the Delaware Bay. I elect not to enter the canal, a shortcut into Cape May. It is fairly long, and speed in it is limited to a painfully slow five miles an hour. More importantly, I want to practice navigating in heavy fog. I will need the skill as we move north, especially in Maine and Nova Scotia.

Just as we pass the canal entrance's defining jetties, visibility drops nearly to zero. My eyes are fixed on the radar screen, and we have slowed to idle speed. I decide to hold a course just off the Cape's beach and follow the coast's outline on the radar around the end of the Cape, then north to the Cape May Inlet, a decision that brings me close to disaster. As we creep along through the heavy fog, I keep a close watch ahead. Suddenly, looming out of the gray soup a rock jetty is upon us, jutting out into the water from the beach. *Rascal* is about to slam into it, but I yank the helm hard to starboard and apply throttle to the port motor, narrowly missing the rocks. My heart pounds as I realize how close we came to serious trouble. I vow to keep a closer eye on the radar, which clearly shows the jetty now on *Rascal's* stern. The chart for this area also shows the jetty, but I failed to examine it carefully enough. The radar and the chart show another jetty just ahead, and we easily steer around this one. My success in avoiding collision and my now closer watch on the radar screen begin to give me a growing confidence in navigating through fog. We easily find the Cape May Inlet, avoiding numerous small boats in the process, and then—blessed relief!—the fog lifts to reveal a beautiful blue, sunlit sky. After refueling in the Cape May harbor, I decide to head offshore toward our destination at Bay Head, thus avoiding the longer, winding route of the ICW with its many slow-speed zones.

The fog has lifted, and the seas offshore are gentle rollers kicked up by a south-southeast wind of five to ten miles per hour. *Rascal* flies over these in rhythmic cadence, her bow gracefully rising then falling. Each time her bow plunges back into the sea, a great lacy spray of water billows from her hull. Our speed and *Rascal's* powerful motors remind me what a good choice she was for this trip. We are on a northerly course a half mile off the beach. It is a holiday weekend and the beaches are invisible beneath their cargo of human bodies. Suddenly, again without warning, we hit another fog bank, this one along the shore near Atlantic City. Using radar, GPS, and the chart, we locate the inlet from the ocean leading to the ICW and decide to head in. It's too dangerous and slow to continue offshore in the heavy fog. As I locate our position, a large performance boat pulls within earshot. He has no navigation gear aboard, but sees *Rascal's* radar dome mounted on the T-top, and asks to follow us through the inlet. We are happy to help. We are several miles from the inlet and proceed cautiously, but find it easily. As we pass through the inlet into the ICW, we leave the fog behind for the moment.

Proceeding north on the narrow, winding ICW, we encounter hundreds of boats of every description, sightseeing, cruising, fishing, playing. The traffic is like none I've seen before, not even in the Waccamaw River at Myrtle Beach. The water boils with boat wakes. At the point where the ICW passes through the Barnegat Inlet, another heavy fog bank rolls in, blinding me in a crowded, narrow waterway. The radar is no help; there are too many objects on the screen. I can't distinguish which are channel markers and which are boats, but we grope our way along, thinking that if this fog lasts through the day and into the night we could be stranded here overnight. Finally, the fog lifts, and I see how far out of the channel we have wandered. I laugh at my luck in these conditions and head north. At the marina in Bay Head, I call my friend Jack, who picks me up and takes me to his cozy new home where I meet his girlfriend, Alice. Jack is finally beginning the long recovery from a terrible case of Lyme disease that went undiagnosed for three years. He was badly debilitated and became depressed, but after finding a specialist expert in the disease, he is now improving under heavy doses of antibiotics.

~~~

The day is cool, overcast, and rainy as we leave Bay Head and pass through the Manasquan Inlet, which marks Mile Zero of the ICW, the last of the protected waterway on the east coast. From here on it will be open ocean cruising, except for New York Harbor and Long Island Sound, until we round Cape Breton at the north end of Nova Scotia and enter the Gulf of St. Lawrence. We head through the Bay Head Canal, then out the Manasquan Inlet in a light rain and fog. The seas, I am thankful to see, are gentle rollers on *Rascal's* stern as we head north, running a half mile off the beach. Shortly, we reach Sandy Hook, which guards the entry into New York Harbor and pick our way through the thin fog under the famed Verrazzano Narrows bridge and into the inner harbor. The fog keeps me from seeing much until we are a half mile or so away, so it is an exhilarating surprise when the Statue of Liberty bursts into view, the Great Lady standing there as she has for over a hundred years, welcoming millions to America. As we near her, the sun miraculously breaks through, and the fog lifts. I bring *Rascal* to a stop at her base and look up at this magnificent monument, as so many have done before. I am inspired and awed.

We press on a short distance and pause again at Ellis Island. To starboard lies Manhattan and the world's grandest architectural exhibition. The two monstrous towers of the World Trade Center dominate this incredible landscape of vertical steel, stone, and concrete.

On this very island during the Revolutionary War, the British General Howe and General Washington marched their two small armies side by side, Washington along Central Park West and Howe along Park Avenue, and neither knew where the other was. They could do the same today, I think, for different reasons.

As the fog lifts, I can see great ships lying at anchor along the south shore of the harbor, waiting their turn at the docks. There is surprisingly little boat traffic. Mostly pleasure boats, some sightseeing boats, and a few ferries ply these wake-churned waters. *Rascal* is by far the smallest boat in sight, but she easily handles the chop and crosses the harbor quickly.

We head up the Hudson and dock at Chelsea Piers. The Piers are a large-scale rehabilitation of old city docks turned into a sports complex. They have become basketball courts, tennis courts, roller rinks, and more. There also is an amazing golf driving range on one of the piers, with the Hudson River on three sides. Around the perimeter of the pier is a gigantic net, perhaps two hundred feet high, to keep the golf balls out of the river. The net at the end of the pier has a sign indicating it is 250 yards from the tee. The tee areas are perhaps fifty yards wide, accommodating twenty or so golfers, but stacked four high as is the practice in Japan and elsewhere when land is costly. A bag of balls is twenty dollars (versus three dollars back home in Jacksonville). There also is a putting green set into concrete, except that the surface is the green sandy material used on clay tennis courts. Strange, I think, the lengths to which people will go to practice golf in a big city.

On the third day of my four-day stay in New York, I encounter a young man and woman in my hotel who recognize from my gear that I am a boater and comment on it. He is a Protestant minister of a church in a village near Lake Constance in Switzerland and also is a sailboater. The large and painfully shy woman is a parishioner and friend. I invite Reinhold and Ingrid to join me on a day trip up the Hudson to the United States Military Academy at West Point. We take a picnic lunch acquired at a wonderful deli near the hotel and head upriver aboard *Rascal* on a breezy, sunny day. At the start of this little excursion, I try to draw Ingrid from her shell. With my abbreviated German vocabulary, spoken with a Southern accent, and universal hand signs, we communicate in primitive fashion. Reinhold speaks fluent English and helps us over the hard spots. Both are new to America and are fascinated, very nearly overwhelmed, by the wild diversity of New York City. In contrast, one could visit, say, Zurich and get a reasonably reliable impression of the rest of tiny, homogeneous Switzerland, but I encourage them not to judge the rest of the U.S. by this one hardly representative city. Happily, they plan to travel the entire east coast.

We lunch while moored in the river at the base of the mighty gray stone fortress that is West Point. After lunch, we tie up at the rough service dock and climb the hill to the magnificent academy grounds, covered in lush grass outlined with massive trees, radiant in the cool summer sun. We admire the statue of George Patton, with his twin revolvers at his waist. An amiable colonel comes by to say that Patton stands facing the library because as a student there he did poorly in academics and never visited the library; now he is consigned forever to make up for it. Eisenhower's statue naturally occupies a special place on the grounds. Reluctantly, we leave this place of gray stone and quiet beauty and have a fine cruise back to New York City. Along the way *Rascal* is briefly challenged by some young men in a sport boat, but they are left in the mist of our wake as I push her to sixty miles an hour.

FOUR

Hurricane Bertha
New York to Boston

LEAVING NEW YORK CITY, we head down the Hudson, past the Great Lady, round the south end of Manhattan Island, then head up the East River to Throg's Neck and Long Island Sound. The Sound on this brilliant summer day is a deep blue, its surface gently rippled under a light breeze. The few sailboats here and there have barely enough wind to fill their sails. *Rascal* flies along easily toward our destination of Port Jefferson. It is a quaint, touristy village. I stay at an inn on the water and tie up *Rascal* in a slip out front. Because dirty rain in New York has stained *Rascal's* gel coat, I spend a couple of hours scrubbing her down and removing the tar stains she has accumulated. When I finish, she gleams anew. At the bar before dinner, I have a talk with a local man, who tells me about this area. Its inhabitants are mostly wealthy New Yorkers who maintain vacation homes here. It is too far from the city to commute. He says it gets extremely cold here in winter but is nice from May through September. It is surely a fine place on this perfect day. At dinner, I watch a brilliant sun as it sets over Long Island Sound and afterwards go to bed, happily exhausted.

~~~

The day is cool and cloudy, with scattered showers. Bad weather is forecast. According to the weather channel on the VHF, the South is alert to the approach of Hurricane Bertha. She may be headed this way. We get a late start and cruise to Plum Gut, where we turn and enter Gardiners Bay, visit Greenport for fuel, and press on. We are headed for tony Sag Harbor, located near the extreme east end of Long Island in what is called the fishtail, after the shape it vaguely resembles on a chart. We dock in a well-protected cove with floating docks, anticipating that Hurricane Bertha may strike. It has come ashore at Cape Fear, North Carolina, with winds of more than one hundred miles an hour. This day's bad weather is a harbinger of things to come. I check into an inn across the street from the marina, clean up, then walk around the town, a former whaling center. At a local bar, I meet two guys from Jacksonville, who are captain and mate on a sportfishing boat out of Montauk at the extreme end of Long Island. We have a good talk about Bertha, boats, and fishing, then I turn in for the night, expecting Bertha sometime the next day.

~~~

The dawn brings gray, ominous skies, some wind and rain, and a falling barometer. I check *Rascal's* dock lines. She is firmly secured to a floating dock and protected from the dock by fenders. The dock now floats about five feet below the level of the wood bulkhead that defines the tiny cove. The docks are attached to fixed pilings by means of strong steel rings that allow the docks to ride up and down on the pilings. Violent winds and water could cause the rings to shear from the docks, but they seem well bolted and the protection of the cove should keep the wind and wave forces in check. Storm surge is the primary concern in coastal waters. I consider what effect it will have. I notice that as the water rises and the floating docks rise with it, the anchor rings could rise right over the tops of the pilings. This would be disastrous because it would set the docks free of any horizontal restraint. On further inspection, however, I notice that the tops of the pilings are somewhat higher than the top of the enclosing bulkhead. This means that the rising water in the cove will spill over the top of the bulkhead before the dock rings slide over the top of the pilings. I am relieved and walk up the street for coffee and a newspaper, then return to my room to read and wait for Bertha.

Despite my previous checks, I remain apprehensive and return to the dock for more thought. What troubles me is that *Rascal's* port side is laid up against the floating dock, against which she could be pummeled. All four fenders are deployed between her hull and the dock, but high winds might flip these back into the boat or on top of the dock where they'd be no use. The dock sits low in the water, the deck of it coming no more than a third of the way up *Rascal's* freeboard. Could *Rascal* be tossed up on top of the dock? Doubtful, but maybe. The solution is to center *Rascal* in the slip rather than alongside the dock. I tie a line from her starboard bow cleat to the dock piling (there is no cleat) of the adjoining slip, slacking the port bowline tied to the dock's cleat. I run the starboard stern line to a cleat on the adjoining dock and slack the port stern line until she sits parallel to both finger docks, centered in the double-wide slip. My risk, a slight one, I hope, is that the rings of the dock in very high water might rise enough to foul the starboard bowline. I doubt this will happen. Now I am pleased with the docking lines; I've rigged them as best I can. I can now only await Bertha's arrival.

For lunch, I walk to a local cafe, and there meet the charming, inquisitive, and loquacious Asha Sangari, a Hindu woman from a wealthy family in India. She and a collection of her friends, including a dentist from Russia, bought a failed restaurant in Sag Harbor and are struggling to make it profitable. They all work in the business. They have families, twelve people altogether, and all of them live in the rear of the restaurant in a kind of commune. She loves America because of the freedom and opportunity it offers to all, but especially to women. Her country's cultural values concerning women are, in her mind, hopelessly backward. She came here at first to be a student, completed three years of medical school, then stayed on. I don't ask why she did not finish medical school. She is childless at age forty-four. Her boyfriend, Richard, works with her in the restaurant. I meet him—tall, skinny, quiet. Asha then starts quoting Hindu philosophy and tells me about the Hindu equivalent of the Golden Rule, mixing all this with trendy environmentalism. She moves on to yet another subject. At last, after an hour and a half of talking, I excuse myself and return to my room for a nap. Bertha is heading our way. Weather is always the crucial wild card in boating. Often it is a great deal more severe, or less severe, than forecast. In this case, Bertha turns out to be not much, winds forty to fifty miles an hour with moderate rain, over by 7:00 p.m.

In the week I have been in New York waters, I have come to like New Yorkers generally. Every person I have encountered has been friendly and helpful. They talk loudly, rapidly, and with their unmistakable accent, but I have grown to like it. It's almost humorous. They tend toward glibness, but the ones I have met are articulate and smart. They have a great sense of humor, making up jokes as they talk, using gestures and voice modulation for emphasis. Outside of New York City, service is extremely competent and the towns tidy and manicured. (Of course, that I have seen only wealthy resort towns on this trip no doubt skews my impressions.) The north shore of Long Island Sound is a high bluff lined with large, beautiful homes, looking across the sound into the setting sun. This would be a fine place to spend a summer, although I wouldn't want to be anywhere near here in winter.

~~~

We leave early. *Rascal* weathered the storm in fine shape, and we are eager to be on the seas again. Today marks the first time we will leave protected waters (except for a few offshore runs with inlets available) and head out into the open ocean. We run along the last of Long Island's north shore, pass Montauk at the end of the fishtail, and set a course for Block Island. As we leave the lee protection of Long Island, we encounter trouble. The remnants of Hurricane Bertha have stirred up the ocean. Huge rollers are coming in from the south-southeast. They are twenty feet high or more and poorly formed. An ugly chop assaults us at the crest of the big waves. I set the trim tabs about halfway down in order not to drive *Rascal's* bow down too hard as she runs over the top and down the back side of these following seas. She needs to be given some slack in the bow so she will not dig into the back of the next wave but can rise with it. As she ascends the waves, the powerful motors strain in protest, churning to drive the boat forward and stay on plane while climbing the bumpy hills. They scream with relief as *Rascal* passes over each summit and surfs downhill.

Many of the troughs are so deep the sky is blocked by huge mountains of water. It feels as if we are about to be run over by monster tidal waves coming at us one after another. *Rascal* tops these waves easily as she blasts ahead. Still, I feel uneasy. The waves are not really a threat, and I know *Rascal* can handle them well, but they are very large and intimidating, and their poor form frequently causes *Rascal* to drop precipitously off a wave top, plummeting more than I expect and leaving my stomach hanging in the air. I feel as if I will come out of the padded seat, so I hold on tightly. These massive waves bring me as close as I have ever come to being seasick. I think it's apprehension combined with the sharp, unexpected drops and the disappearing horizon that causes the queasiness. Still, by concentrating intently on what I have to do, I ward off the growing turmoil in my stomach. My mouth gets dry, but I soon calm myself and focus on the job at hand. In rough seas, I continually have to catch the nautical charts as they slide off the console top, where I keep them for quick reference. This has always been a problem, a nuisance really, but today the charts somehow catch a blast of air and nearly sail off the stern. They fly into the transom and luckily are caught there, so I slow and recover them. Without these, I'd be in trouble for sure.

Block Island looms into view, surrounded by a churning, hostile sea, a high, bluish-gray lonely mass across the horizon. At its southern cape, huge breakers crash onto the ancient rocky shores, and massive atomized flumes of exploded water burst into the sky. A distant fog bank shrouds the seas but seems to end at the cape. The fog isn't moving our way. As we gain the lee of the island, the seas calm, my taut nerves relax, and I easily find and enter the well-protected harbor, much like Ocracoke's but several times larger. This weathered place, it seems, could have looked fifty years ago exactly as it does today.

After breakfast, my composure regained, we head out to sea again, this time for Newport, Rhode Island. The seas continue massive, threatening. We get to the mouth of Narragansett Bay, where the rollers encounter shallower bottom that forces them upward and closer together. They become steep walls of water but close enough together that *Rascal* spans them, easing the ride. We head up the west passage of the bay in calmer inland waters, round the island that defines the two passages, and head down the east passage into Newport. Everywhere there are sailboats, all kinds. Here a unique, sleek old schooner, there a 12-meter racing sloop and a 100-foot, three-masted yacht from England. The harbor is packed, yet some of these large boats are under full sail, weaving in and out of the hundreds of moored boats. It is a spectacular sight. We take our time and circle the harbor, seeing old Fort Adams, the splendid old mansions, the former New York Yacht Club, the Ida Lewis Yacht Club, and more.

I have decided to stay the night here rather than go on to Nantucket. The VHF weather channel tells me offshore winds near Cape Cod, where we would go, are thirty to thirty-five miles an hour and seas are ten to twenty feet. I know these are giant rollers and are threatening but not really dangerous. Still, there is a small craft warning, and I am not anxious to battle these big babies for a few more hours. Winds and seas are expected to lie down tomorrow. I eat dinner at the White Horse Tavern, established in 1673, the oldest tavern in the U.S. Then I wander. The town is touristy, but not tacky. It is a well-executed rehabilitation, and in some places, a reproduction of a New England whaling town, with all the usual shops and bars. A heavy fog rolls in, giving the night lights an eerie glow, particularly the lights of the many sailboats in the harbor. And a strange quiet envelops the town, except for the periodic forlorn bleat of the local foghorns. I sit on *Rascal* to enjoy the night, and the owner of a neighboring boat stops by to talk. He is a local and tells me the fog will not lift until about noon tomorrow. He is quite pleased that his wife is encouraging him to buy a large boat and is happy to have such a wife. We finish our talk, say farewell, and I turn in for the night.

~~~

Beginning in 1629 and ending abruptly in 1640, some 80,000 men, women, and children migrated to the New World from a few counties along the east coast of England. They fled religious persecution, economic depression, and disease. Initially, they settled in Massachusetts, then spread to other parts of New England, including here in Rhode Island. These people were the Puritans. A deeply religious Protestant sect, their folkways included a closely shared set of community standards rigorously enforced. Liberty was not something an individual enjoyed on his own; it was a limited public concept. Individuals willingly subjected themselves to numerous confining restrictions imposed by active local government. They also received from their government protection from economic deprivation through, for example, the so-called poor laws of the time. A strict work ethic was ingrained and enforced in their communities. The Puritans could actually be convicted of a criminal offense for wasting time. The idea that time is money was Puritan in its origin. The essential folkways of the Puritan Culture still exist today (though altered by time and the subsequent influx of peoples from other cultures).

Puritans are the foundation of the modern Yankee culture. As Professor McWhiney writes in his *Cracker Culture,*

> "*Observers from the 1600s through the 1800s agreed that as a rule Northerners and Englishmen were industrious and business-minded farmers, traders, and manufacturers who were persevering, profit-oriented, enterprising, often cold and stiff, sometimes rude and greedy.*" (p. 245)

Compared to southerners, Yankees were more urban, less violent, better educated, more even tempered. They readily accepted the need for government control and regulation of their lives and communities. They willingly paid taxes to support government control. Reflecting this preference for central authority over their lives, Professor Fischer notes in *Albion's Seed,* New England state and local governments, consistently over more than three hundred years, have taxed their citizens more than twice as much as those of other regions. It would be difficult to imagine an American culture whose values were more dramatically different from those of the Warrior Culture.

~~~

Morning arrives wrapped in a thick blanket of fog. At times, I cannot see the other side of the harbor, and the wind is blowing hard. The weather channel on the VHF in the dockmaster's office says winds are south-southeast at twenty-five to thirty miles an hour with gusts to thirty-five and forty. Seas, largely driven by the winds, are six to eight feet. Both seas and winds are projected to increase later in the day. A small craft advisory is in effect. I am disheartened, but wait for the fog to burn off. I read and write, stroll about the waterfront, then rent a cab for a town tour. The driver is well informed and delivers a fine historical account of Newport. The great mansions are splendid, some sitting on large lots. Some are open to public tour, others have succumbed to redevelopment— in one case a hotel, in another a condo project. I guess the heirs of these places would rather have the cash from these enterprises than continue to bear the high cost of keeping up the mansions. Newport's downtown commercial area consists of either beautifully restored old buildings or new ones designed with good taste that fit nicely into their surroundings.

At the center of town are narrow streets, designed originally for horse-drawn carriages, lined with lovingly cared-for wood clapboard houses dating from the late 1600s. They look just as they did in those earlier times. The driver points out the birthplace and home of heroic Ida Lewis, for whom the yacht club is named. She was the keeper of the lighthouse that stood on a tiny rock inlet in the harbor and, one night during a violent storm, went out in a small boat to save the lives of six men. She thus destined herself to receive the eternal thanks of Newport's people by having her home memorialized and a yacht club named for her. The clubhouse is on the same rock where once stood the light that Ida Lewis tended. It is an inspiring story of simple bravery and a community's gratitude.

We drive along the magnificent Ocean Drive and through Brenton Point State Park, past stunning scenery. We are on rocky cliffs that today are enveloped in a thin, vaporous fog. It could be the California coast at Carmel, Pebble Beach, or Monterey. Below, the wind-whipped sea crashes relentlessly onto the shore, sending forth great plumes of spray. The shoreline is jagged, with points of land jutting defiantly into the angry sea, each adorned with an elegant home. The homes' owners have chosen their building lots well. Newport is an important historic center. It has fully a third of all the existing eighteenth-century buildings in America. It has the first street illuminated by gaslight. It has the oldest church in America and the oldest synagogue. Its main urban concern is adapting its compact size and narrow streets to the modern automobile. On these streets, gridlock is easily achieved. Parking is nearly nonexistent, and the hordes of tourists, though they drive the economy, are a mixed blessing. In spite of all its problems, this is a delightful town.

All too soon my tour ends, and I return to the docks to visit *Rascal*. I imagine that she is as eager as I am to cast off the lines that bind her and once again charge eagerly into churning seas. I ask the dockmaster about the offshore seas, which are hidden from our view by the high ground that protects the harbor. Three sailboats that had left earlier in the day have called on the radio to say the seas are too rough. They are giving up and returning to the harbor. I greet two of these at the dock and they report steep, confused waves that are too much for even these experienced sailors to handle. Still, I think it may be possible. Traveling at *Rascal's* speeds, it would take less than an hour to get to Menemsha on Martha's Vineyard, and we have taken on worse seas together, *Rascal* and I. In the dockmaster's office are two professional boat captains swapping stories. One, Eric, declines to leave the harbor even though he is running a modern sixty-four-foot motor yacht. The other has just come from Edgartown on Martha's Vineyard but had a rough, wet ride—in a ninety-seven-foot motor yacht. With great reluctance, I decide to stay over a day and wait for the weather to clear. I am disconsolate at this setback, yet I know it's the right decision. Eric and I tentatively decide to head out together tomorrow morning. If I follow him, the mass of his bulky motor yacht will crush waves and leave a relatively smoother wake, but *Rascal* would have to travel no more than ten miles an hour. This could prove frustrating. I'll wait until dawn for the final decision.

~~~

The day begins with a brisk wind from the south and the early signs of a cloudy sky. There is no fog and I am elated. After I have breakfast and check out of the hotel, it is still early. I am eager to be under way, so I leave word for Eric that we won't be following him. Just as *Rascal* is leaving the harbor in the morning sunshine, a thick, cool fog rolls in and visibility drops to perhaps a hundred yards. Without hesitation, I decide the hell with it, we have good navigation gear and radar. We're pressing on. We run to the number two sea buoy in fierce rollers right on the bow, then turn east. The big, poorly formed waves are directly on *Rascal's* beam. Roiling chop is intermingled with the rollers. *Rascal* is getting kicked around badly. I set the trim tabs lower, thus putting downward force on the bow and pressing more of the boat's hull into the water. She responds well. I have stopped the slamming, although with more of her knife-edged hull digging into the water she is more susceptible to being knocked off course. I watch the compass and bring her back to our chosen heading. We encounter sea buoys along the route indicating we are right on course, but I frequently stop and use the GPS to double-check our position along each leg.

As we enter Buzzards Bay, just west of Cuttyhunk and Nashawena Islands, we pick up some lee protection and the seas begin to subside. We find our way in the cold, dense fog through the narrow pass between Nashawena and Pasque Islands, then cross Vineyard Sound into Menemsha Harbor. Menemsha is quite small, a quaint village with a beautiful west-facing beach famous as a venue for watching sunsets. After a short break from the cold fog, we head northerly along the Martha's Vineyard west coast to Oak Bluffs, where we secure a boat slip directly on the boardwalk in front of the Wesley Hotel. The Wesley is an old, eighty-four-room, classic Cape Cod hotel that fortunately has room for me. After settling in, I rent a small motorbike and realize that I must look faintly ridiculous, with a black pot-like helmet perched on my head as I tool about the island. But, ridiculous or not, tool I do.

If there is a word to describe the several villages of the Vineyard, it would have to be "tidy." Uniformly tidy. Oak Bluffs is beachtown ugly, yet beautiful still. The small boat-filled harbor is faced ashore by quaint, gingerbreaded cottages, dating back to the mid-1800s. The road to Edgartown runs along a picturesque beachfront with a salt lagoon on the other side. It is the most tidy of the villages. All its houses seem freshly-painted white with black shutters. A few have faded cedar shingles. Small, colorful gardens adorn most homes, and some have hand-laid stone fences. I visit the wharf and gaze across the Chappaquiddick Canal, then ride out to Atlantic Beach. The place is cool, foggy, and breezy, facing into the prevailing southerly winds, and crowded. I stop to ride a red 1941 Waco airplane, but because the fog is rolling in, the pilot is unwilling to fly. I drive through West Tisbury, stop for ice cream at the charming rural village of Tisbury, then head back to my hotel to read, write, and prepare our course to Nantucket.

After dinner, I wander around Oak Bluffs. The cottages at the harbor are part of 330 built originally to accommodate participants at a Methodist Campground Meeting site begun in 1835. Each is covered in its own unique version of gingerbread and painted brightly. They surround an old church and steel-roofed dome built to hold revivals. I walk away from these cheerful cottages admiring the exuberance they express, albeit uniform and orderly, and the ardent devotion to their faith that led the people to congregate here. It is a cool, starry night with a light breeze ruffling the leaves of the great oaks. I return to *Rascal* and am invited to join three guys on a neighboring boat. We have a lot of laughs and enjoy the night air together.

~~~

As we are preparing to leave, a young couple from Montreal on a neighboring boat ask if they can follow us to Nantucket. They are without any navigation gear. Why they would be here without charts or the first piece of navigation equipment is not apparent. He has a thirty-foot high-performance boat with blaring exhausts. We cast off with the help of my three companions from last night and head out of the harbor for Nantucket about thirty-five miles away. The day is cool and windy. The skies are clear, but the seas are rough and on our beam, making the ride bumpy. *Rascal's* starboard motor runs intermittently on five instead of the usual six cylinders. It is the same engine that was a problem in North Carolina. She has power enough, but I'll have to get the problem fixed.

Nantucket has a large, well-protected harbor that is filled with boats anchored, docked, and under way. We get two slips for the day, and I and the couple from Montreal go our separate ways, agreeing to meet again later in the afternoon for the trip back to the Vineyard. The island of Nantucket is generally low and rolling. It is mostly scrub with scattered stands of small short-leaf pines. The soil is sandy, evident on the many unpaved roads outside the town center. I wander around, then visit the Nantucket Whaling Museum. It is my good fortune that a lecture begins just as I arrive, and I am enthralled by it. The speaker stands in a large room of an old brick warehouse that serves now as the museum. The room is filled with the artifacts of whaling; visitors can just walk up and handle them. It gives them life and meaning beyond the museum. He relates in detail how whales are hunted and, when found, how six men in a longboat—an actual one of which sits next to the audience—stalk, harpoon, tire out, then kill the whale. From his talk, it is easy for the audience to imagine that we are there on the five-year voyage around the world as whale after whale is dragged back to the mother ship and rendered, mostly for its oils. As he talks, I am astounded once again at the travail, the risk of life, the arduous, unceasing labor, the sacrifices that ordinary men will endure for economic gain. After the lecture is over, I walk through all the marvelous exhibits, astounded at the harshness of life then. I think how sweet and gentle it is now by contrast.

I rent a convertible and go for a spin around the island. The inner parts resemble an English moor: wide spaces gently rolling, covered with low, green grassy scrub. Elsewhere there is a farm, extensive forests, and a confusing network of sandy, rough one-lane roads. Homes are scattered widely. Nearly all the buildings on the island are clad with weathered cedar shingles and show the same basic architecture, varying only in size and shape. The trim color is, with few exceptions, white. If the culture of a people, their heritage, is revealed in their buildings, these people are mostly descended from the Puritans of Massachusetts. For the people of Nantucket, uniformity and conformity are important. They willingly give up small but important freedoms, for example, to choose the style, color, and building material of their homes, for the sense of belonging to a community with strong internal relationships. They sacrifice for the greater good because they believe, as did their forebears, that life lived in a strong community with internal consistency and shared values is superior to life as an individualist who values freedom from influence by others. These people of Nantucket, and their ancestors, are ascetic and deeply conservative. They resist pretension and decoration. There are no neon signs, not one traffic light, no fast-food outlets, no franchised retailers. The small, utterly charming seaside cottages in the English-like village of Siasconset, where I stop for a pleasant lunch, are attractive, have nice gardens; they are clean and, always, tidy. They are all nearly alike emphasizing uniformity and conformity. Nowhere is there a hint of exuberance, brashness, audacity, self-expression, self-indulgence, sensuality. These are anathema to the people of Nantucket. Soon enough it seems a bit boring to me— charming, wonderfully livable, but boring.

The Montreal couple greets me warmly at the dock. I like them. Because they will go back to Oak Bluffs and I to Edgartown, they follow me until they are close to their destination and then we part ways with fond farewells. I hope to see them in Montreal.

It is Regatta Week in Edgartown, but I find a slip in the haul-out area of a marina and check into the Daggett House, a mid-1800s home of a sea captain, now divided into rooms for rent. Mine is a nice one, with its door opening onto a small garden. The room is not air-conditioned but, with open windows and a small fan, it is pleasant. I go looking for a place to eat a light meal with a view of the Edgartown Harbor. I find just the place. Its second floor has an outside deck where I can watch dusk settle in over the lovely waters now filled with sailing boats. I meet a couple from Annapolis. He is an apartment developer recently retired, and she has worked for their local symphony. We have a pleasant talk, enjoying the night air immensely, until I decide to challenge her on the issue of taxpayer subsidies generally and those of symphony orchestras in particular. Quickly she becomes irritated and defensive. Her position on orchestra subsidies is that (a) "it's the arts," offered as an argument that settles the issue; (b) it's small change, and; (c) there are lots of other subsidies. Her mind's obviously made up. Her husband is amiable and both are very nice people. I choose not to press the discussion. We part as friends. Then, just as I sit down inside to eat, serendipity strikes. It turns out that this bar is the annual summer venue for a ten-man section of the Yale Glee Club, called the Vineyard Sounds. They perform, without subsidy, for an hour and a half. They are terrific. The house is full and the audience, including me, is spellbound—a fitting end to a fine day.

~~~

This day dawns as the nicest yet. There are no clouds, only cool, dry air. I am excited and eager to be going. The next destination is Boston, and my forbearing wife, Kitty, will be meeting me there. The dockmaster wishes me well and we're off. We leave the harbor at Edgartown and make for the cut at Woods Hole, passing the eponymous Oceanographic Institute, heading north to Buzzards Bay and into the Cape Cod Canal. The seas are smooth and the ride is a delight. Just as we are about to exit the north end of the canal, we get a surprise. Suddenly, dramatically, we hit a wall of cold air. The temperature drops by at least fifteen degrees. This, I learn, is caused by the water beneath *Rascal's* hull becoming, in the space of few feet, far colder than it has been. We have reached the end of the warm waters influenced by the Gulf Stream and the beginning of the cold, dark waters of the North, chilled by the Labrador Current. I stop to put on long pants and a heavy jacket. Looking down, I see the water is clear but, for some reason I don't understand, it is quite black, and its blackness gives it a malevolent, gloomy appearance. I become uneasy, but today these forbidding seas are glassy smooth, and despite my fears, we have a delightful cruise along the Massachusetts coast into Boston Harbor. The coast here is mostly high bluff, dotted with homes much like a good deal of the eastern seashore north of the Delaware River. The population is densely packed into a small geographic area, and many want to live on the water, seeking the joys that arise from long views of open water.

We enter Boston Harbor as many have done before. The harbor is dotted with numerous small islands, several bearing old fortifications that attest to the strategic importance of the place. It is busy with ship and ferry traffic; there are some huge wakes to contend with. If I do nothing about oncoming wakes, *Rascal* will launch off the first wave and land with an awful crash that, it often seems, threatens to scramble the internals of the delicate onboard electronics, to say nothing of my own. When I can spot the approaching wake in time, I quickly lower the trim tabs to their maximum and apply full power. The combined effect forces down *Rascal's* sharp bow, causing it to slice the wake rather than getting launched over it.

We pick our way along the channel markers, closely following the charts, and approach Rowe's Wharf at the heart of downtown Boston. There I am greeted warmly by my wonderful wife. We have been apart now for nearly a month, and I'm happy to see her standing there on the dock, a broad smile across her face. We walk along the attractive, historic waterfront and spend some time at the local aquarium. We go for a slow cruise out of Rowe's Wharf, through the harbor to the old part of the city called Charlestown, where Old Ironsides is now docked. We make a respectful pass by her, then enter a lock, exiting into the Charles River. On this warm, summer day, the river is alive with sailing prams zig-zagging back and forth, close hauled against the wind. Gently, we pick our way through this chaos and continue upriver past several of the boathouses for local university crew teams. The Charles is like a wide boulevard passing through a scenic part of Boston. Across from Boston, on the Cambridge side, are the gracious old buildings and glitzy new ones of the M.I.T. campus and the Harvard Business School.

On the return from our idle-speed cruise, we visit Charlestown again. This is the site of one of the most famous river crossings in American history. Paul Revere and the Whig leaders of Charlestown on the other side of the Charles River had worked out a contingency plan for warning the countryside of any impending British expedition. If Revere, through his spies, knew the British were coming by land, a single lantern would be displayed at night in the steeple window of the Old North Church. If they were coming by sea, two lanterns would be displayed. Late on the night of April 18, 1775, Thomas Bernard, Robert Newman, and John Pulling, acting in concert with Revere, went to the church. There, Bernard stood guard while Newman and Pulling climbed the 154 stairs to the steeple window, opened the shutters and displayed two lanterns. The Whigs in Charlestown knew the British troops would be leaving Boston by boat to Cambridge. At 10:15 p.m. that same night, just before the lanterns were shown, Paul Revere walked out of his home and down to a wharf in the North End, where he met Joshua Bentley and Thomas Richardson. All three climbed into Revere's little boat, shoved off, and with muffled oars began rowing north toward the Charlestown ferry landing. The sixty-four-gun HMS Somerset was anchored across their path, swinging on the incoming tide, armed sentries fore and aft. Revere and his accomplices would surely be spotted in the light of the full moon that night—except that, miraculously, on that night the moon hung low on the horizon, its light blocked by buildings, leaving Revere's boat hidden in dark shadows. The three men crept by the great warship and made it to the ferry landing. There, Paul Revere mounted a sturdy, fast mare, named

Brown Beauty, and set off on his ride into destiny. *Rascal* now idles slowly, reverently, over the same waters of that historic crossing.

FIVE

Rocks, Rocks Everywhere
Boston to Camden, Maine

IN THE MORNING, Kitty leaves to visit our energetic son staying with his cousins in Providence, and we cast off and head north. Today is as ugly as yesterday was beautiful. I am amazed at the sudden change. It is gray and cool, with wind-blown rain and heavy fog. Visibility is about a half mile, allowing us to cruise at normal speed. As we turn north and head toward Cape Ann, *Rascal's*, starboard motor begins to malfunction, acting just as it did back in North Carolina, losing power and dropping RPMs intermittently. I suspect it may be the same part gone bad as before. (It will later prove to be an engine computer called the Electronic Control Unit (ECU), that directs the ignition of the fuel-air mixture on my carbureted engines.) The fog is thick and the wind-whipped seas are rough. A small craft warning is in effect. In the harsh conditions, the fog makes me feel isolated, very much alone. I can't see land, other boats, anything at all but the cold, dark, roiling, gloomy waters. These are unfamiliar waters with exposed rocks, islets, and shoals lurking about. I stop *Rascal* every ten miles or so to study the chart and our position on it because I can't read while being knocked around underway. I need to be sure we are on the right course, not headed for disaster. The small displays of the instruments and the tiny print on the charts are jostled so roughly that they are only a blur.

Strangely, I welcome the foul weather. It gives me the range of sensory experiences I seek. It is always challenging. I curse it and fight it and suffer from it, but deep down I love it. This is my private battle with Mother Nature: "Come on, baby. Gimme your best shot." It is, of course, best not to get too cocky. "Nature bats last," as the fan's sign said in Candlestick Park just after the Loma Prieta earthquake stopped the 1989 World Series. Still, the confrontation is great fun.

We crash through the seas by the austerely beautiful lighthouse and attached outbuildings at Cape Ann on rocky Thacher Island. We pass close by the island, making certain to avoid a shallow rock shoal nearby. Just past the light, we change course and make for the village of Rockport. It is enveloped in fog, yet still picturesque as we pass through an opening in its breakwater. In an instant, we leave the punishing seas to enter the flat, womb-like calm of a harbor. Boats are moored here in safety. There is a small wood-frame building that houses the Sandy Bay Yacht Club, and a tiny inner harbor with high bulkheads that hint of the big tides here. The two dockmasters of the yacht club show me where we can tie up, and then they help me try to find a mechanic. No luck. Gale warnings are now in effect. Judging from the terribly rough seas I've just come through, I should have known that, but I failed to listen to the weather reports. The truth is that, except for the approach and aftermath of Hurricane Bertha, I have not listened to the weather channel at all. It's not that it's not useful. It surely is, and the forecasts are generally accurate. It's just that I want to confront whatever weather and seas exist each day, no matter how rough they may be. If it's too rough, I can always turn back, though I haven't yet. This is not the approach recommended by texts on seamanship, it's not the cautious approach, and it's not mine customarily. But on this trip, with *Rascal* beneath me, it is the one I will take. Anyway, with *Rascal's* speed, we can duck into a safe harbor quickly. I decide to head to the larger town of Portsmouth, New Hampshire, about 28 miles farther, where I may more easily find a mechanic.

In driving rain and a rough following sea, with gale warnings posted, I head due north, and I make it to Portsmouth Harbor only to be greeted by dense fog. Once inside the harbor I become completely disoriented due to the lack of visibility and take some time to regain my bearings. At last, after aimlessly puttering about in the harbor, we find a marina—well, a dock to tie up to. At one end of the dock is an ancient, 100-foot-long steam-driven tugboat called the *John Wannamaker*. After tying up *Rascal*, I meet the tug's owner, Walter Dunfey. Walter lines up a mechanic who can look at *Rascal's* motor, first thing Monday. It is Friday afternoon, so I am stuck here until then. With the gale-force winds outside I'd probably be here anyway, so I resolve to make the most of my stay.

Walter is in his mid-forties and is a casual, smiling guy. He bought the tug and refitted her with two fancy bars and two floors of fine restaurant. He built the floating docks, which are attached to pilings at a bulkhead, behind which are condos, an office building, and an inn where I stay the night. Walter is an entrepreneur. It took him two years to get all the permits he needed from the city for his tug/bar/ restaurant, but in the end, he prevailed. He and his intense wife, Julie, operate the business, and it has been slow getting off the ground. I hope his business makes it. He has invested all of his own money, borrowed more, and taken great risk to see a vision become reality and to earn a profit in a completely new venture. The bar has a warm, cozy feeling and is crowded this night with friendly, talkative people, including a lady from Montreal and her son and daughter-in-law. They are delightful people. There are lots of others, including two married ladies in their forties here for a rowing competition. I am happy to have found such a pleasant place to spend the evening. The weather outside is hostile, with the wind blowing fifty miles an hour as a cold front passes through.

~~~

Because the inn I stayed at last night is booked for tonight, I move to the Oracle House, built in 1702 and recently remodeled. It is just across a narrow street from Prescott Park, on the Piscataqua River. The river, I learn, is the second fastest flowing river in the U.S., after the Columbia. It speeds along at six to ten miles an hour, depending on the season and rainfall. The Oracle House is run by Heidi, a pleasant, plump young woman who is rightly proud of her domestic skills. She is a helpful hostess. I walk around Portsmouth's historic area, with its many shops and restaurants, see the famous Naval Shipyards, then rent a car and drive north up 1-95 to Kennebunkport, Maine. The traffic is amazingly dense, going both ways, three lanes each. The highway is a giant parking lot at least five miles long, and at Kennebunkport itself, there is still more traffic, every vehicle trapped among narrow, winding village streets lined with the ubiquitous too-cute-for-words shops.

At last, I get on Ocean Drive, with its fine old New England- style mansions. There is a tiny, solemn Episcopal church, built of local stone, that sits on a manicured point of land guarded by weathered rocks, onto which the wind-whipped seas crash violently. The church sits stoically, silently, as it has for a very long time, resolute against the raging weather. It is a lovely spot, tranquil even on this harsh day. I spot a group of tourists standing along the roadside waving. I look in the direction of their affections in time to see former President George Bush and entourage drive by. His family home, or compound, is a large, imposing, perfectly Maine-coast affair sitting proudly on the tip of its own peninsula, called Walker Point. After still more traffic, far too much of it, I get back to the inn in Portsmouth, eat dinner, and turn in early.

After some reflection and sufficient firsthand experience, I find only two objections to life here in the North: the cold winter and the high population density. The place is cold and snow-prone from about November through April, a full six months of near uninhabitability. The locals complain, agree it's too harsh, but live here anyway, at least until they can afford to move south. The other six months are delightful, with cool, dry days, light breezes, lush, dark green, feathery soft grass, radiant skies, and big leafy trees. Colorful flowers bloom everywhere in carefully tended gardens. This is a place where, after a hard winter, Nature bursts forth in all her glory, furiously and intensely expending all her energy in the few precious months of warmth, before the climatic door slams shut once again. Into this wondrous landscape fit snugly the ever-tidy New Englanders. Their homes, even those of the blue-collar class, are clean, freshly painted, Colonial-style, mostly clapboard, and adorned with the requisite brass door knocker or carriage lamp. Conformity, orderliness, cleanliness are everywhere to be found, seemingly self-imposed as the only way to survive the harsh winters.

There seem to be far more people in any given area of land here than elsewhere, perhaps exceeded only by Europe. As a result, the narrow, winding streets of the towns and villages, designed for horse-drawn carriages, are often choked with traffic, and parking is difficult. Driving on the modern highways can be frustrating, especially on weekends, when a good portion of the population all head for the same few small coastal towns. There are almost no pickup trucks, battered old cars, or flashy new ones. Even the vehicles are clean, neat, nondescript. The herd instinct is apparent. Density has its virtues, however. The towns are highly social places with people milling about, shopping, dining, drinking. There is a communal feeling, of necessity, and people are helpful to each other and show finely developed social skills. I have not yet heard angry words or seen an ugly disposition. These surely are here; I just haven't seen them.

Psychologists have found that people in the North achieve slightly higher cognitive test scores than those in the South. Intuitively, I can sense the difference as I pass through here. Nearly everywhere, people are quick-witted, competent at their chosen tasks, well-informed. It results in things working better. Life is less bothersome for everyone. While people are brighter, they are also more communal, sharing a set of social values that promote conformity, the virtues of labor, thrift, and concern for the welfare of others. The Puritans have left their mark. For all of this New Englanders pay a price in the loss of some of their individuality and personal freedom. There is little self-expression. Vivaciousness is hard to find. The people are almost too well behaved. Still, this would be a wonderful place to live—about six months of the year.

~~~

I awake to a bright blue sky, cool, dry air, and a brilliant sun; winds are not the forty-five or fifty miles an hour of yesterday but are still high, maybe twenty-five. I eat a light breakfast in the sun-washed garden of the inn and work on a few business matters. Life is good at the moment, and I relish it.

I take the car along the coastal highway south to yet another too cute, historic restored village—Newburyport on the Merrimac River. After lunch, I eat an ice cream while seated on a shaded park bench in a village pedestrian mall and watch the people. They are generally attractive. There are very few tacky T-shirts with obnoxious slogans or commercial propaganda. Most people wear collared shirts; colors are muted. Few males have long, shaggy hair. I see no tank tops and, amazingly, almost none of the ubiquitous, oversized, clompy sneakers. There are a lot of fine-looking families, many with three generations represented in their group. Hardly anyone is grossly overweight. There is no boisterous behavior. Conversation is at normal volume. There are no drunks, and nobody is even drinking, at least on the streets. This, I observe, is very different from the Warrior Culture of the Deep South.

Driving along the shore, I come to a beach. It is a narrow stretch of sand several miles long, between road and sea, and it is swarming with people on this sunny, cool, breezy day. Reasonably enough, there is not a person in the water; it is far too cold. These people just come here to enjoy the sun, the view of the ocean, and each other. There are no billboards and all the other signage is so uniform it must be heavily regulated. It leaves a pleasant impression on the mind to drive along without garish signs bleating their messages in your face. There are few gas stations and stores and those few seem to fit in with the rest of the landscape. I think of the array of laws, rules, regulations, ordinances, permits, licenses, and bureaucracy it must take to impose so much conformity, but here it is imposed on a willing constituency.

Surely, some must complain at the margins, but order is what most want, and get.

I like Portsmouth. It was settled by the English in the early 1600s. They named it Strawberry Banke after the plentiful wild berries they found growing on the banks of the Piscataqua River. Most of the town burned in 1803 and was rebuilt. It has been revitalized over the past twenty years and has a plethora of shops and restaurants common to the many other historic towns and villages of New England. The difference with Portsmouth is that the town is comfortably frayed, worn at the edges. It is lived in. The buildings look used. Walking the streets, I feel I could be in the mid-1800s, not in an ersatz, Disney-like, architects' rendition of that period. There is nothing precious about the place. It has a wonderful little town square—well, not a proper square, geometrically speaking, more an important intersection that is cockeyed in a pleasing way. At its heart is a fine old church (as one would expect in Puritan New England) on whose steps sit some scruffy youngsters dressed in peer-approved attire. On the corner across from the church sits a delightful cafe and bakery with sidewalk tables, where young couples, families with children, older couples, and students all mingle easily.

This is a twenty-four-hour town. Lots of people actually live in town in lofts remodeled from old warehouses, in tiny apartments on the two floors above the shops, and in genuine New England saltbox houses crowded happily together on narrow, winding streets. Many date from the mid- to late 1700s, having escaped the fire, others from the early to mid-1800s. And of course, there are newer homes, though none that could remotely be called modern, and a few newer, if bland, modern buildings in an inoffensive scale. This variety of architectural periods gives the town a charming, rumpled look. There is still uniformity of a sort, but it is vague, subtle, as though not planned by some omniscient urban planner or trendy architect.

For all, it's New England Puritanism, Portsmouth has—gasp— a tattoo parlor that, from casual observation, does well among daughters of the more affluent (teenage rebellion being what it is), and a bar popular among the Harley and black-leather set. It happily lacks almost all of those tiresome mall stores, the ones whose logoed products make everyone look so much alike. The town's Prescott Park on the banks of the Piscataqua is casual and moderately tattered. Walking through it brings the same sort of familiar comfort we get from wearing old shoes. The Park's fluffy rows of colorful flowers in full bloom delight the eye. This evening the local repertory company is giving an outdoor performance of *The Wizard of Oz*. Townsfolk arrive with lawn chairs, their children babbling with anticipation. The Park's marina is filled with boats here for the weekend from nearby towns. The spirit of a community is everywhere I look, and I like it very much. One day, I'd like to return here.

~~~

This day begins as one of the best yet, a brilliant sunlit day with a cloudless sky and smooth seas. After getting the Electronic Control Units I need from the local marine repair service that Walter Dunfey directed me to, we head out of the same harbor entrance that we entered just a few days before in a thick fog. Now, with visibility, I see that it is rocky and beautiful. I also see how close I came to great piles of rocks, and cringe at the thought of what might have happened. Perhaps it is well I didn't know what soon was to happen. We make the short run out to a tiny group of islands called Isles of Shoals and look around. This is where early English seafarers set up a tightly knit community to support their fishing ventures in the New World. They even predated the Pilgrims' landing at nearby Plymouth Rock. (The Pilgrims didn't actually land at Plymouth Rock; they landed on Cape Cod and later migrated to Plymouth.) On one of the Isles sits incongruously a huge wood hotel built perhaps in the 1920s. It is in some disrepair, but, judging from the small crowd milling about its grounds, I guess it is still in operation. A local later tells me it is owned by a religious organization. We then head back to the mainland and enter Little Harbor at New Castle Island, where I refuel and have lunch, then cruise a short distance along the coast both north and south of the harbor and return to Prescott Park Marina and the room at Oracle

House Inn. I am eager to be on my way after a delightful four-day layover in Portsmouth and hope tomorrow's weather will be as fine as today's.

~~~

It isn't. The day is badly overcast, cold, and rainy, but at least there is no wind and the seas are calm. We will go to Boothbay Harbor on the first of about five days cruising the magnificent Maine coastline. The steel-gray sky seems to envelop us, casting a gloomy pall as we head north along the coastline and round Cape Elizabeth. Visibility is reduced, hampering any sightseeing, and what islands I can see loom into view out of the gray miasma, never fully revealing their detail.

This coastline is like nothing else I have seen. There are no more sandy beaches, only rocks, islands, islets, and more rocks everywhere. The sea seems to have grown colder and blacker. Harbor seals frolic here and there, reminding me, as if I needed reminding, that we are in the cold, northern seas influenced by the Labrador Current. The shoreline is heavily forested with fir, spruce, and pine growing out of black, sodden soil. On this ugly day, everything is wet from the cold drizzle and damp fog. My sockless feet are cold, as are my hands and face. This is July. What happened to summer? We wind our way among the countless islands, visit Jewell and Eagle Islands, head up the Kennebec River to Bath, then down the Sasanoa River, cross the Sheepscot River, and enter Boothbay through Townsend Gut.

Maine is different and so is Boothbay. The state is rustic, almost primitive. Its people are rural folk for the most part. The town is a jumble of fine old homes, converted into wonderful B&B's and inns, mixed badly with unsightly three-story modern motels jutting into the harbor. Most of its shops are confined to just a few blocks along part of the waterfront. They are tacky. The restaurants are simple places in need of repair with menus that lack imagination. Except for the attractive homes, B&B's, and inns, in one of which I spend the night, I do not care for Boothbay and will not be back.

~~~

The morning brings more dense fog. It is hard to see across the harbor. I refuel and, in doing so, meet a fascinating man. He is a retired Navy officer and Naval Academy graduate, resident of Orr's Island, Maine, and a classic, yet gregarious and humorous Yankee. He regales me with funny stories, relevant Bible quotations (though he clearly is not a devout believer), and some of his and his family's sailing adventures. His lifetime friend soon joins us. He is also a charming character and served as the judge who decided the America's Cup dispute between the U.S. and New Zealand. I am captivated by the good humor and close friendship of these two and later regret not talking with them longer.

I return *Rascal* to her slip at the marina and there replace all six of the Electronic Control Units on the starboard motor. Because of a manufacturing defect, some of these units fail when the motor is under heavy loads, causing one or two of the six cylinders not to fire properly. Power drops as a result. Though I am not adept at mechanical work, I nevertheless complete this task with a sense of accomplishment.

Finally, the heaviest fog lifts and we head out into the haze for Camden. After an hour, the fog thickens again and with radar, GPS, and the charts, I pick my way slowly along the channel markers to our destination at Camden. Even in the heavy fog, it takes only a few hours to get there. The outer harbor is jammed with boats of all descriptions, including several fine sailing yachts here from other countries. The tiny inner harbor is also packed cheek by jowl, but I find a slip at the town docks and check into a nicely restored inn. I have come to prefer inns, which are mostly old mansions, restored and converted to hotel rooms. The rooms are generally large, with high ceilings and modern baths, and their decor is nearly always more agreeable than the bland functionalism that characterizes modern hotel rooms offered in small towns everywhere. The place I have chosen is a block from where *Rascal* is docked and in the heart of town.

~~~

For the past two days, the weather has been awful, and we are confined to port. The fog is so heavy that I can barely see across the small harbor. A constant, soaking drizzle falls, making everything clammy, and it is cold, forty-five to fifty degrees Fahrenheit.

Undaunted, I wander around town taking stock of the place. Despite the ugly weather as a backdrop, Camden has its charms. Its commercial area, like Boothbay's, is confined to just a few blocks near the waterfront but, unlike Boothbay, it is not utterly given over to tourist shops and bad merchandise. Instead, it blends the needs of its visitors with those of its citizens and does so in a homey, old-fashioned way. Many of its fine old homes are now converted to inns that stand proudly side by side along tree-lined avenues, competing eagerly with each other for the favors of travelers. I reflect on the marvels of entrepreneurial capitalism that has taken dilapidated, worn-out, family homes, whose owners have died off, moved away, or fallen on hard times, and given them a new life in pursuit of profit, making them available to the traveling public and giving their guests a taste of grand living if only for a night or so. These entrepreneurs are a dynamic element in these traditional New England communities and add a needed richness to the fabric of life. They help to transform tired old mill towns and fishing villages into delightful places with a new vitality. Thanks in large measure to these people and their vision, Camden is a thriving community.

I rent a car and drive to Owl's Head and there visit the remarkable Transportation Museum. Founded by the former chairman of IBM and son of IBM's founder, the museum is a quirky place not unlike a great garage housing a family's various playthings, keeping them well preserved over the years. The "garage" is a steel, industrial building that smells faintly of motor oil. There are many old cars, airplanes, and motorcycles, with their attendant paraphernalia. Some are bizarre, flimsy contraptions, others, like the 1934 Ford Coupe and the old Cord and Duisenberg, graceful reflections of genius and ingenuity, all lovingly restored and maintained. It is a very special place, and I am enthralled. Interestingly, I learn there are three more such museums close by and guess they too were begun by wealthy men who summered in the area and collected cars as a hobby to the later benefit of us all.

I also visit the Penobscot Marine Museum in Searsport, Maine, at the head of famed Penobscot Bay. It is here that I see the most astounding film I have ever seen. In 1929, young Irving Johnson left his home on a farm in Massachusetts to pursue his dream of a life sailing the high seas. Luckily for us all, young Irving recorded this amazing adventure on a motion-picture camera. In 1980, this film was transferred to a modern videotape with narration by the then-aged Captain Irving Johnson. I watched this tape, utterly awed.

It is not an easy matter to train for the sea living in a sea of corn stalks, but Irving was inventive. He climbed, descended, and climbed again, many times over, a tall utility pole to simulate a great mast, and while at the top he imagined the pole to be swaying violently in a storm-tossed sea, a triumph of self-deception. To practice his balance and to steel himself against any fear of height, he stood on his head at the peak of the pole. He was a young man determined to excel in his chosen craft. It was not for Irving Johnson to work in comparative ease on board a steamship, then prevalent. He wanted a great adventure on a magnificent sailing vessel, so he signed on as a raw, untested seaman aboard the mighty *Peking,* plying commercial cargo between Hamburg, Germany, and Santiago, Chile. He could not have chosen a better ship. She was 378 feet long and displaced eight thousand tons. Square-rigged with 350 separate lines and four monstrous masts reaching up seventeen stories, she carried more than an acre of canvas when fully deployed. She could reach speeds of more than seventeen miles an hour.

The *Peking,* with Johnson aboard, left Hamburg and promptly encountered seventeen consecutive days of merciless storms in the North Atlantic, where the great ship was tossed about like a chip of wood. He and the ship survived this only to greet the dead calm of the mid-Atlantic doldrums, where no air stirred for weeks. Johnson wanted to sail in mighty storms, to invade them on his ship, confront and master them. He got more than he had hoped for in the frigid waters of the South Atlantic near Cape Horn off South America's southern tip. Sailing head-on into the prevailing westerlies, the *Peking* was greeted by a monster storm with winds up to a hundred miles an hour and waves reaching eighty feet high. It would be a feat of heroic scale merely to cling to a ship in such conditions, but Johnson and his shipmates, led by their stalwart captain, didn't merely cling. They climbed the ratlines, ascending the giant masts, and furled the huge sails while the ship tossed wildly, the mast tops with men attached swinging in a wide arc. Seas crashed onto the *Peking*'s decks, washing overboard anything or anybody not firmly secured. Two men were washed over, never to be seen again. And through it all Johnson's camera rolled, capturing in real life this amazing drama. This amateur film, imperfect by modern standards, is a simple, brief adventure narrated with intense feeling by a person who survived it.

I walked out of this tiny film room with its picnic-like folding chairs, out of the tiny museum, into cold drizzle beneath a steel-gray sky, and I felt the exhilaration Johnson must have felt on this voyage I had just shared with him. He was a man who knew how to live a full life and live it well. I admire him for that. After a short cruise on *Rascal* to the classic Maine island village of North Haven, we return to Camden, concluding what has been a wet and dreary but still uplifting day, thanks to Irving Johnson.

SIX

Disaster
Camden, Maine, to Eastport, Maine

THE FORECAST WAS FOR CLEARING SKIES today, but I awake to find overcast. Nevertheless, I have had enough of town life, and I am eager to move on. As *Rascal* eases out of the Camden Harbor into Penobscot Bay, the fog becomes thicker than ever. We pick our way slowly and carefully along the tortuous route to Bar Harbor, dodging rocks, nearly running into a lobster boat, and making a course around islands that go by us on the radar screen unseen in the grayness that envelops us. As we near Mount Desert Island, on which Bar Harbor is located, the sun at last, after too many days, shines on the spectacular coastline of this area. We round the south end of Mount Desert Island, turn north between a neck of it and Great Cranberry Island, and head for Northeast Harbor. It is a long, narrow bay surrounded by steep, wooded hillsides. We slowly cruise the harbor, then leave it and run close along the south and east shores of Mount Desert, headed for Bar Harbor.

The shores of this island, the Acadia National Park, are magnificent. Mountains up to fifteen hundred feet high, covered in fir and spruce with bald rock faces jutting out through the forest, dominate the skyline above the bay. It is at the summit of Cadillac Mountain in Acadia National Park that each day's dawn sunlight first falls on the United States. The shoreline is dramatic and boulder strewn, with the black, cold water crashing onto the rocks. Here and there mansions dot the landscape at sea level. We pick our way through the Porcupine Islands, then turn into the shore at Bar Harbor. I am elated; this is the cruise I have sought. After a quick lunch in Bar Harbor, we take off. I am full of enthusiasm as we head southeast across Frenchman's Bay toward the south end of Schoodic Peninsula. Just a few miles later, the skies, seeming to taunt us, again turn to dense fog. In a fateful decision, I elect to press on anyway, hoping as always for better weather ahead.

My purposely chosen method of navigating *Rascal* lacks precision, especially in fog, and for that reason can be troublesome. The captains of most larger, slower, and deeper-draft vessels, when in unfamiliar waters, employ their GPS units to establish a series of consecutive electronic destinations, called waypoints. These are identified from the chart as lying in good water and frequently are the precise location of a specific channel marker. Waypoints are described by their exact latitude and longitude, often expressed down to hundredths of a nautical minute, equivalent to a few feet. Once waypoints are entered into the memory of the GPS, the unit will tell the captain such useful information as how far he is from the waypoint, what compass heading to steer to get there, how far he is off the direct track from the last waypoint, and more. All that remains is for the captain to follow the directions given by his GPS.

Simplifying matters still further, he will often employ an autopilot connected to and taking orders from his GPS to set and hold the proper course, thus freeing the vessel from the extemporaneous, impulsive, or whimsical command that can lead to disaster. The autopilot is particularly useful in dense fog, where the absence of any fixed reference points confuses the mind and can lead to a sort of nautical vertigo in which the vessel is steered in circles while the captain is certain he is proceeding on a straight course, though the compass tells him otherwise. Thus, absent the entry of erroneous waypoints, the GPS, or GPS with autopilot, is a nearly foolproof device. But, alas, it has its shortcomings, particularly in the special case of a small, fast boat, like *Rascal,* operating amid the winding water courses of the Maine coast. The legs between waypoints in a tortuous waterway are numerous and quite short, requiring the tedious process first of determining the precise coordinates of each channel marker, then of entering these into the unit's memory. *Rascal* travels so fast that she would complete these legs in short order, a few minutes or less. It is often simpler, no more error prone, and quicker to use another method.

While I use GPS and autopilot on longer open courses, I prefer, partly for reasons of temperament, what can be best described as seat-of-the-pants piloting when operating in heavy fog along short courses. It works like this: first, I determine the next mark I want to hit, usually a channel marker; then by looking at the compass rose imprinted on the chart, I determine an approximate heading, making sure to avoid obstructions shown on the chart. I then take off in that direction, frequently consulting the compass to be sure I'm roughly on the desired track. I also frequently consult the radar screen to help me avoid other vessels, keep away from nearby land, and confirm with reference to nearby land masses that my approximate heading is correct. When I am in the vicinity of the channel marker, I use the radar to help me locate it exactly. I pull alongside it to verify visually by its markings that it is the one I seek, then proceed in like fashion to the next, and so on. A good case could be made that my technique is so imprecise as to be dangerous and consumes more time and effort than entering a long series of waypoints. That may be so, but my technique has the overriding advantage that it heightens the sense of adventure, requires all of one's senses to work well, and is great fun—at least until this afternoon.

The courses between channel markers along this part of the Maine coast are much longer, and over these longer distances, my seat-of-the-pants technique grows increasingly inaccurate and the case for waypoints more compelling. Engrossed in the task before me, I fail to shift to the more precise technique. I become frustrated in my efforts to locate the first marker buoy off Schoodic Point by the images of several sailboats that resemble channel markers on the radar screen. I promptly head for the boats, only to realize my mistake and dart off in another direction, looking for the quarry. At last, I find the channel marker lurking in the miasma off the tip of Schoodic Point. I turn for the next checkpoint, a rock ledge five miles away. This we find by nearly running into it, but spot it through the fog in time to avoid it. Now we set off on a two-and-a-half-mile course in search of a buoy marking a narrow passage through the dangerous Petit Manan Shoals. Again, we are frustrated in our efforts to find this buoy, and the fog has grown thicker still. The radar screen shows nothing, perhaps because I am not yet a proficient operator and may have it tuned poorly, perhaps because the buoy is outside of the short, half-mile range I have selected.

Using the GPS, I locate our position on the chart and that of the buoy, establish a heading to get there, and set off in that direction, going much too fast for the conditions. Visibility is only some thirty or forty yards. I am glued to the GPS, radar screen, and charts, while also watching ahead and operating *Rascal's* controls. I have throttled *Rascal's* motors up so we are now fully on a plane, traveling at about thirty-five miles an hour.

Then it happens. Through the mist, I can just see water breaking over the low-lying granite rocks of Petit Manan Shoals that now rush toward me like the bared teeth of a sea monster. Instantly, I drop the throttles to neutral, then try to slam them into reverse. *Rascal* drops off plane, but for some inexplicable reason the transmissions fail to shift into reverse and *Rascal* continues onward, slower now, but steadily, sickeningly, toward the rocks. Surprisingly I am relaxed; my mind works clearly and quickly. I am certain that we are going too slow for me to be killed or seriously injured. *Rascal* will be damaged, but probably not me. I know there is nothing I can do to avoid the inevitable.

With an awful grinding, scraping sound, *Rascal* strikes a partly submerged ledge of rock, which she slides over with ease until the foot and propeller of one motor, extending deeper into this granite lined water than her hull, strike the ledge hard, kicking the motor up and shredding the prop and the lower unit of the motor, leaving only a jagged aluminum tail where the gear housing and prop had been. We lodge fast in a small pool between the submerged ledge we just crossed and a low pile of menacing rocks just a few yards ahead. *Rascal* is being knocked about by wind and waves, absorbing harsh jabs against the hull. Because she is extremely well built, I am certain the hull has not been penetrated.

After assessing the damage, I decide that the now incoming tide poses the greatest threat. The increasing wind and waves will combine with the tide to force us higher and more roughly onto the rocks, increasing the chance the hull might be holed, sending me into the black, freezing water where I could not long survive. But, ironically, the tide is also our friend. If I could stabilize our position using an anchor and wait for the tide, we would then have a chance to float over the entrapping ledge and at least avoid the chance of sinking. I call the Coast Guard on the VHF, giving them our position from the GPS; I describe our situation. After some preliminaries, they dispatch a boat to rescue us but estimate it will be thirty to forty-five minutes before it arrives. Thinking that might be too late, I try to heave *Rascal's* anchor off the bow beyond the ledge, but I can't get it out far enough, nor can I get it to take hold on the smooth surface of these rocks.

At this moment of dire need, a local man, Clint Holley, fortuitously arrives on the scene. After we hit, I noticed a small skiff anchored on the backside of the shoal, but nobody was aboard or in sight nearby. As I look that way again, here comes Clint rowing a tiny inflatable dingy toward us. He had been collecting seaweed along the lee side of the rocks and had heard the collision. As he draws near, he yells to us with an impish grin across his face, saying with typical Maine understatement, "You're in a bad place." I agree and with his help quickly work out a plan to get *Rascal* stabilized and off the rocks. After tying two fifty-foot sections of extra line to the anchor line, I pass the anchor to Clint, who rows it out beyond the ledge and drops it, tugging at it until finally it catches hold. Then I haul on the anchor line, moving *Rascal* slowly to the ledge and get the bow pointed into the wind and waves. The quickly rising tide soon increases the water depth enough that I am able to pull her over the ledge and into the deeper water. Clint stands by in his little dinghy until the Coast Guard is in sight, departing with a friendly wave and my grateful thanks.

I am chagrined and humbled by our near disaster, all the more by the humiliating experience of being towed into Northeast Harbor behind a Coast Guard rescue vessel. On the way, I reflect on how easily it might have been much worse. Had we come along a short while later when the higher tides just covered the rocks, we surely would have crashed into them at a speed high enough to tear the bottom out of the boat, with possibly fatal consequences. Had Clint Holley not been gathering seaweed along the rocks that afternoon, we could have been pounded into the rocks and sunk by the rising seas before the Coast Guard could arrive. Indeed, it could have been much worse. Clint told me he knows of eighty-eight sunken wrecks in the waters around these shoals, and the Coast Guard said I'd be amazed at how many times they have pulled boats off these rocks. Still, it is painful. I will hereafter use GPS waypoints for courses over a few miles in the fog, and I will not negotiate dangerous waters in heavy fog at high speed. These are hard lessons I have learned, and they will guide me from here on.

~~~

It is a glorious day of blue skies, sunshine, and cool, dry air, the day I have been long waiting for, the kind that fills Maine summers with throngs of tourists. It is a cruel irony that on this perfect day for cruising, *Rascal* lies in the harbor, badly damaged. Worse yet, the forecast calls for this fine weather to end by Wednesday, the earliest day I could return to the sea. Somehow this seems like just punishment for my poor judgment. Yet I do what I must and promptly call to arrange for *Rascal* to be hauled and for a marine repair shop to assess her damage. I take a cab to see *Rascal* for myself in Northeast Harbor. When I arrive, she has just been lifted from the water and is slung above the ground between the frames of the lift vehicle. At a distance, she looks proud and defiant, her prominent bowsprit thrust out like the rock-solid jaw of a professional boxer. But, as I walk closer, I can see that her gelcoat—the shiny outer surface of her fiberglass skin—has been badly damaged by the unforgiving granite rocks. Ugly wounds are scattered over her hull below the waterline and on the bow stem, where she absorbed the first and harshest blow. In places, she is so badly damaged that the lamination under the gelcoat has been penetrated. If not repaired, this will allow water to seep into the layers of the lamination, causing more extensive damage.

As she sits there, trundled in the sling, she pours water from her bilge drain at the transom. I check closely and find that the saltwater intake mounted on the transom below the waterline was jarred by the collision, breaking the watertight seal around it and allowing water to leak into the bilge. This too must be repaired, along with the serious damage to the lower parts of her motors. There is no doubt that we'll be laid up here for at least five to six days, more if the needed parts are not readily available. I issue the appropriate orders for the work to proceed. There is not the slightest thought of ending the voyage. I will not turn back. My place for now is here, seeing to the repairs, and, when they are complete, we'll press on. Oddly, I am not disheartened by these events. I greet them as obstacles to be surmounted, a test of my will to carry on. I will focus intently on the tasks at hand until they are complete and then be off.

~~~

The best estimate now is that I'll be here in Bar Harbor for at least a week, so I rent a car and make plans to travel around the area. Each of the towns I have visited along the way is unique, a complex tapestry of people, places, history, and resources, each with its own subculture and its own economy. Most grow—or, failing to grow, change or stagnate—haphazardly, with no guiding vision of their future, though often with a keen attachment to their past, celebrated in a plethora of museums and quasi-historic displays. Their town governments, reflecting more or less accurately the wishes of their constituencies, react to events as events assault them. They pass laws or make rules or grant or withhold permits and licenses or assert their police power, all without much idea of where it all may lead.

Bar Harbor is such a town. It has a colorful, unique history and is surrounded by a stunning landscape, yet somehow it has gone badly awry. Walking around this small town, I can sense what happened. Zoning rules were relaxed to allow quiet, old neighborhoods filled with families to be transformed into busy groups of B&Bs and inns. Each sale of a family home to an innkeeper was a purely voluntary and rational transaction. The home became more valuable as an income-producing inn once the zoning was changed to allow it. But what was rational between buyer and seller was a slowly spreading, debilitating condition for the town. The balance between the commercial demands of tourism and the stabilizing effects of local, permanent residents was upset, resulting in the overcrowded, traffic-choked tourist town of today.

Compounding problems, it appears that signage and architectural controls were relaxed so that now a pedestrian confronts a hopeless jumble of visual noise, hanging or perched at all levels, lighted variously, each shouting to be seen. Most shops have, in addition, sandwich boards, window signs, and garish flashing signs placed as visual barricades about the premises. The hapless tourist, assaulted by this chaos, cannot assimilate much information. The eye is overwhelmed. The mind shuts down in self-defense. What remains of Bar Harbor is hardly a town at all, but a large outdoor shopping mall with overnight accommodations. The natural features are still stunning and the wonderful old homes—now B&Bs and inns—are still elegant and lend a needed sense of permanence. The town's history makes for an enchanting backdrop. But the foreground is a lost opportunity and a lesson for towns everywhere.

Tiring of Bar Harbor, I drive toward the charming but busy few streets of nearby Northeast Harbor and on the way stop for lunch at the delightful old Asticou Inn. Sitting proudly on a bluff high above Northeast Harbor, the Inn commands a magnificent view of the long, narrow harbor thronged with boats riding calmly at their moorings.

The Inn, like many of the boats below, is built of wood but has been, also like the boats, lovingly cared for and today looks and feels as it did when it was built more than a hundred years ago. After lunch, I drive the famous Loop Road of the Acadia National Park. I am thankful to see, on this foggy, damp, cool day that this park is not as thronged with people as are many of the National Parks in summer. The part of the road that winds along the shore on cliffs above the crashing sea below is a sensory treat. A thin veil of fog gives the cold, black sea and the hard gray rocks below an eerie ghost-like quality that mesmerizes with its foreboding. This is a scene to enjoy looking at, but not inhabit permanently. Nature here is too aloof to be welcoming. Its harshness is a warning.

From the Loop Road, I make my way along the coast roads until I come to the village of Seal Cove, barely more than a few stores, restaurants, town library, and post office. It is a quiet place, very quiet. There are fine homes built in the traditional Maine style hidden in the conifer forests that line the craggy coast. These, like most of the larger homes along the shore, are the summer homes of the well-to-do from elsewhere. I guess they are contemplative people who come here to read books, take redemptive walks through the forest and along the rugged shore, listen to classical music, dine well, sleep well, and escape from the heat and hurly-burly of the outside world. It is a fine place for all these.

~~~

In a rented car, I board the ferry MV *Bluenose* for the six-hour voyage from Bar Harbor to Yarmouth, Nova Scotia. The trip, all in heavy fog, is uneventful. (The *Bluenose* has since been replaced on this run by a giant catamaran called *The Cut.* It is the fastest car ferry in North America. The trip now takes three hours.) From Yarmouth, I travel north along the easternmost coast highway, stopping briefly at Shelburne and Lockeport. Both are small fishing villages. They are tidy, clean, and have fine commercial harbors. Interestingly, I note that their homes for the most part face inward toward the village rather than outward toward the harbor or sea. Apparently, the people here do not share the idea, common elsewhere, that a view of the water is a desirable amenity. Perhaps, I think, this is because the sea for them is where they work; viewing it from their homes everyday would be like an office worker having a house that overlooked a sea of desks. Or maybe it's because the sea for them is a harsh and dangerous place, not the thing of tranquil beauty others may regard it to be.

One of my missions on this road trip is to tie down once and for all the question of where I can buy gas for *Rascal* along the way. Telephone inquiries have yielded a variety of contradictory results. I have been told, with comforting assurance, that: (a) after all, there are some large towns along the way and, surely, they have fuel; (b) the fishing boats use fuel and I can buy it at their docks; (c) as a last resort, a fuel truck will come to any dock and I can buy directly off the truck. I learn from a fuel distributor in Shelburne that there is no gas in town available at dockside. He says it must be carried in five- or ten-gallon cans from an automobile service station. Because I often need 150 gallons at a time, this clearly is not a practical alternative. He also says a recent change of government regulations has prohibited delivery of gasoline to dockside by truck, although diesel fuel can be delivered in this way. I drive around Shelburne and try to spot a dockside gas pump. No luck. In Lockeport, a village smaller than Shelburne, I am not hopeful and begin to despair, but as I drive out onto a concrete pier to which fishing boats are docked and look across the harbor, I spot a fuel pump. Upon inspection, it turns out to be a single gas pump and its owner agrees that when *Rascal* and I come this way, he will sell me gas, even though I do not possess the required commercial license (another small triumph of capitalism over government regulation). He tells me that almost all fishing boats have diesel engines, so gasoline pumps at dockside are rare, but I get lucky in Lockeport.

I drive to Halifax on the two-lane highway out of Yarmouth, through endless tracts of scrub conifers, revealing either a dry climate, unlikely here at ocean's edge, or poor soils or even poorer conservation practices. Halifax is for the Maritime Provinces a major city, its population combined with that of Dartmouth, its sister city across its harbor, reaching just over 180,000. It is an attractive place oriented along the high banks of a natural harbor said to be the second largest in the world. Its buildings sit low against the skyline. Its homes are clean and well kept, with small yards, most with flower gardens. Except for the traffic, the place feels like a small community. The city slopes gently down toward the harbor's edge, where the waterfront is lined with restored historic buildings, the obligatory maritime museum, shops, restaurants, and a few Canadian Navy vessels on display. There are a surprising number of people walking about on this fine, sunny day, all seeming to enjoy the apparently rare treat of a fogless day.

By prearrangement, I meet my good friend of many years, Jack Burnell, at a Halifax hotel. We go for a walk along the waterfront and plan our travels for the next few days. We talk of his upcoming marriage to a tall, attractive, and talented artist, his children from his first marriage, and a few business matters. We were to meet here, with me on *Rascal*, and cruise Nova Scotia together. But my collision with the rocks has made that impossible. We both regret that we won't be sharing a cruise aboard *Rascal*, but we will make do with a car trip.

After dinner, Jack and I find O'Carroll's Bar, featuring a trio that performs traditional Maritime folk music. All three sing well and frequently harmonize *acapella*. One plays a fiddle; the other two play guitars, one alternating with a mandolin or banjo. The music is a mix of Irish ballads, English seafaring tunes, and Irish ditties with some Scottish music thrown in. The fiddle plays an important role in all their music. The lyrics of many tunes seem to be uniquely from the Loyalist tradition of the English settlers in the Maritime Provinces. One song celebrates the role of Halifax and nearby towns as home port to privateers encouraged by the British to capture the vessels supplying goods to the Colonies during the Revolutionary War. The crowd is a mix of age groups. Both genders are about equally represented, and the people come from all over the Maritimes, some from elsewhere in Canada. Jack and I are the only Americans. I am astounded to learn by watching that nearly all the crowd knows the lyrics and the music to most songs, and they sing along, making gestures more or less coordinated with the music. Here is a very close-knit culture with shared values that span many years. I try to imagine a corollary scene in America and cannot come up with one. Songs are sung and beer mugs raised until late in the night.

The Maritime Provinces of Canada are the tiny stepsisters of the larger and more populous provinces. Nova Scotia is an amalgam of French Acadian, Scottish Highland, Irish Catholic, and English Loyalist heritages. Each co-exists easily with the others, actively carrying on its cultural traditions. Driving along the mostly two-lane highways, we pass in a short distance through Scottish towns like Lake Ainslie, Scottsville, and Dunvegan; then Acadian towns like Cap le-Moine, Grand Etang, and Chéticamp; and Loyalist towns like Yarmouth, Liverpool, and Halifax. The Irish, though widely prevalent, seem not to have many identifiable town names, but there is a Londonderry.

Throughout Nova Scotia, the people are plain, genuine, and uncomplicated. Expensive, stylish, logo-laden clothing seems not to have made its way here. There is no litter or graffiti anywhere. Large U.S.-style billboards are nowhere to be found. Except for the gas stations and a few fast-food places in the large towns, national franchise retailing is not omnipresent. Major intersections of major highways are surrounded by nothing more than trees. The visitor here can imagine that Nova Scotia today is much like a rural American state a half-century ago.

~~~

We drive on a cool, sunny day through the countryside of Nova Scotia to the Strait of Canso, separating the mainland from Cape Breton Island, then north up the Cape to the resort village of Baddeck, which we will use as a base for our explorations, on the magnificent Bras d'Or Lake. Nearby is the summer home of Alexander Graham Bell and in the village a museum of his life and work. Tomorrow we will drive the road we have both eagerly anticipated, the fabulous Cabot Trail, all 187 miles of it.

We get an early start and head northwest along the Cabot Trail through mountainous country that resembles the Scottish Highlands in its topography, though this displays more green and less granite. We greet the coast of the Gulf of St. Lawrence in Acadian Country at Belle Côte and travel north along the coast through tiny villages that, not by accident, resemble those along the Brittany and Normandy coasts of France. Homes here, as everywhere in Nova Scotia, are modest, without ornamentation but always neatly kept. Each town has at least one small, old church, always clapboard, always white, often with black trim, a proper steeple usually with a bell, and always prominently sited as if to better remind the parishioners of their moral obligations. Some are truly beautiful works of simple architecture.

At Chéticamp we wander through an exhibit of terrible paintings by a local artist, reminding us how even the tiniest community seeks to celebrate artistic expression. The locally-made hooked rugs for which this town is famous are interesting and well crafted. Genetically, they're not unlike the chenille bedspreads one occasionally sees gilding car hoods and clotheslines in *alfresco* roadside boutiques in the rural south, hawked by rustic tobacco-chewing entrepreneurs. To be honest, I wouldn't want to live with one of the hooked rugs, or chenille bedspreads, or rustic entrepreneurs either, for that matter. We move on, climbing ever higher on the coastal escarpment of the Cape Breton mountains. Today the Gulf of St. Lawrence below is a limitless expanse of featureless, glistening azure with not a ripple to be seen anywhere. Somewhere off in the distance, water and sky join at an invisible seam, so perfectly matched are their colors. Around the next bend, and higher still, we are above Pleasant Bay, where a school of pilot whales feeds on bait fish. They are so far below we can identify them only through binoculars. We climb still higher, at last reaching the summit. The panorama is like none I have seen before. I think this is what the Rocky Mountains would look like if they were surrounded by the sea.

Reluctantly, we descend from the heights to a tiny harbor with a small collection of colorful fishing shacks. At the end of the rocky road leading out of the harbor toward White Point, we stop the car and walk a mile or so uphill to the edge of a high, barren hill whose seaward edge is a series of small coves gouged by the sea and formed by high, jagged rock cliffs. Waves far below crash into these coves, disturbing the clear pools of cold water held fast within enclosing rock ledges. As I look out to sea, there, not more than a few hundred yards offshore, is a mother whale and her calf slowly trolling for their lunch. We watch until they, seeming to tire with our gawking, leave by diving out of sight and swimming away hidden beneath the surface. We are pleased with our good fortune in spotting these whales, and leave this lovely, barren place wishing we could stay longer. After still more majestic scenery, more than our minds can adequately cope with in one day, we return to our base in Baddeck.

We drive to Halifax along part of the Marine Drive on the eastern Atlantic shore of Nova Scotia's mainland. Boulder-bounded bays, hewn by the black oceans relentless scouring, line this coast. Around each turn in the road lies a new scene. It is as though we are peering into nature's kaleidoscope. Each bend in the road brings a new frame to dazzle the eye. This is a primitive area. There are few towns or villages, and the ones we find offer few amenities for travelers worn out by endless beauty.

Every area that attracts tourists has its set stage postcard piece that serves as the backdrop for its tourism promotions. Peggy's Cove is Nova Scotia's. Jack's otherwise commendable, if sketchy, tourist guidebook warns us away, but we are trapped on a road from which there seems no escape, so we grit our teeth and visit the place, braced for the worst. We are pleasantly surprised. Yes, there are crowds too large for this tiny wayside and there is the mandatory gift shop, two stories of it crammed with gewgaws, brick-a-brack, schlock, knickknacks, dust collectors all. The village's freshly painted lighthouse has by now been the photo backdrop for millions of tourist snapshots. Nevertheless, Peggy's Cove is worth the visit. The topography is much different from any we have seen in Nova Scotia. It is a moonscape of granite boulders strewn haphazardly across a tundra-like plant surface that forms a thin green veil over weathered, deeply fissured rock. There are no trees, no shrubs; ocean pools punctuate the scenery. I imagine that the coast of, say, Labrador far to the north would look like this. I am unprepared for it here. The too-cute lighthouse and crowded gift shop notwithstanding, we are glad we came here. Guidebooks can't always be trusted.

~~~

Jack and I say goodbye and wish each other well. In a few days, he'll be married in a small ceremony in New York. He and his fiancé have chosen well; I think they will have a happy life together. I drive to Yarmouth, board the *Bluenose* bound for Bar Harbor, and arrive there about 10:00 p.m. I start looking for a room, expecting to find one easily, but it turns out the last few days of sunshine—in sharp contrast to the weeks of cold and fog— have brought a horde of tourists to the area. There are no rooms to be had on all of Mount Desert Island or in any nearby town. With no alternative, I sleep—or rather toss about trying to sleep—in my rental car, something I haven't done since I was a teenager. I hope not to do it again.

~~~

I visit *Rascal,* and the repairs are coming along well. She is beginning to be seaworthy once again. Eager to leave, I work on plotting the course we'll travel for the next few days, noting fuel stops, overnight stops, and routes. Carefully, I note rocks and shoals.

Paul Bowden has done a superb job in getting *Rascal* repaired. His fiberglass specialist is a craftsman who does his painstaking work with care. By sanding and filling and matching colors well, he has patched all ninety-eight places where *Rascal's* hull was damaged by the granite. In places, the damage went beyond the skin into the sinew that holds her together; he repairs it all. As she looks now, it is impossible to tell that she has ever been damaged, so smooth and shiny is her hull. Paul's mechanic has removed the eviscerated lower unit of the damaged motor and replaced it with a new one, and Paul and his crew have done a nice job cleaning and polishing the hull and decks. *Rascal* gleams and looks ready for action again.

She is loaded onto a special trailer that will handle her size and weight and is delivered to the marina and launched. She easily passes her sea trial, and at long last, after grateful farewells to Paul and his crew, we set out to sea again—thirteen days after my foolishness gave disaster its opportunity. Now we are speeding across the water once again, leaving behind that ugly encounter. Such relief and joy to be at sea again! To make it even better, the day is made in heaven. We take up a course first to Schoodic Point. The last time we were here, the place was covered by a thick cloud of cold fog. Today there is brilliant sunshine. We cruise past Moulton Ledges and back to the point of our misadventure at Petit Manan Shoals. In the sunshine, I elect to run simple compass courses and easily locate the needed channel markers. When we arrive at Petit Manan Shoals, I stop and study the chart carefully. Two fairway buoys establish a path across the treacherous rocks lying just below the surface at high tide. The cruising guide says to cross the shoals by passing close to the buoys. The terrible experience we had here has made me fearful of this place. My mouth is dry. But rational faculties tell me I have done all I can to select the proper route, so I ease *Rascal* back up to speed and fly close past the markers and over the shoals without incident. Sometimes guidebooks *can* be trusted.

Blessed relief. We are at long last back on course, covering new ground. We weave our way through a patchwork of offshore islands, head for Moosabec Reach, then run close by the town of Jonesport. Suddenly, a light fog closes in. Visibility is still good enough that we are not endangered, but the life-giving, warming rays of the sun are shielded by a dull gray mist. This depresses my spirits and casts a pall over the world around me. There are no longer any colors, only gray and black. The sea, as always in this part of the world, is latently evil, icy cold, and black. Beyond Jonesport, we come to Rogues Roost, a horseshoe-shaped lagoon, well protected from harsh seas and graced with spectacular scenery. The few passes through the rocks guarding the horseshoe are narrow and rough, with breakers crashing into the rocks on either side, but I follow the chart carefully and work my way into the lagoon for a look around. Inside the horseshoe, the water is calm but still black to the gray shoreline. Even the rare beach ringing the curve of the horseshoe is today a shade of gray. I am sure that in the sunlight this is a beautiful place, but now, with a light rain beginning to fall and such light as there is waning in the late afternoon, it is anything but inviting. I decide to press on.

At Brothers Island Passage, the inside course takes us west of Cross Island, through the Narrows past Old Man Rock, then out into the open ocean. Seas are running three to four feet, but they are on our starboard beam, constantly trying to knock *Rascal* off her heading. We are running a few miles offshore in order to avoid any shoal area, and I cannot see through the fog more than a few hundred feet. The radar displays the outline of the otherwise invisible coast. We progress along the fifty-mile shore and locate the sea buoy offshore of the village of Lubec Narrows. Here we leave the ocean and pass into Passamaquoddy Bay behind Campobello Island, the summer home of President Franklin Roosevelt. The tide rips through the Narrows at a fearsome pace, but it is no match for *Rascal's* power. We break free of its grip and tie up at the fuel dock in Eastport.

Eastport lies on the coast at the mouth of the Bay of Fundy, which has the highest tidal variation in the world. At certain times of the year, the drop from high to low tide exceeds fifty feet. It regularly is in the thirty- to forty-foot range. Tidal bores can be so severe that they cause big waves, like whitewater rapids. In the summer people regularly shoot these rapids in motor-powered inflatable rafts. The reasons for the big tides are complex but have to do with the length, depth, and cross-section of the bay and how these relate to something called tidal oscillation. These tides, needless to say, offer unique challenges to the boater, especially one from comparatively tideless Florida.

Because of the tidal variation, Eastport's fuel dock is unique. It is a rectangular wooden box that floats at water level and is attached by heavy steel rings to thick wire cables. These cables are strung vertically, one end firmly secured to huge concrete blocks sunk into the bay's floor, the other attached to the top of a fixed wood pier that, at low tide, is thirty feet above the water (think of a three-story building). The pier is a latticework of wood pilings rising from the bay floor interlaced with cross beams for lateral support. As the tide rises and falls, the fuel dock floats up and down on the cables. It is my misfortune to arrive on this scene at low tide. As I tie *Rascal* securely to the floating dock, I hear a voice and look up, way up. Thirty feet above me, a man with a bald head looks over the edge of the pier and passes down the extraordinarily long fuel hose.

When *Rascal's* gas supply is replenished, I look up, hoping the man with the bald head will be coming down the ladder with a portable credit card machine in hand. No such luck. Instead, he motions for me to come up the ominous-looking ladder that, I soon discover, has cold—everything in this part of the world seems cold—steel rungs made slippery by the sea growth that attaches to them while submerged for hours every day. Boating is my thing. Climbing slick, three-story ladders is not. And I have a confession to make: for all my nautical boldness, I'm terrified of heights. With serious misgivings, I start up. About halfway, I become focused on the fiendish facts of climbing ladders: to progress, it is necessary to let go of one rung with one hand and grasp the next, and to move one foot from one rung up to the next. Done at low altitudes, it is easy to move both a hand and a foot at roughly the same time. This leaves, for an instant, just the other hand and foot as the sole attachment to the ladder and all that stands in the way of disaster. But at higher elevations, where I now find myself, this clearly reckless procedure, with only two limbs attached to the ladder, if only for an instant, is out of the question. Instead, I reluctantly release a death grip on one rung with one hand and grasp desperately for the next, imposing a death grip on the new rung. With the other hand, I do the same. Only now do I move first one foot up a notch, then the other. This technique means that I am always attached to the ladder by at least three appendages, one short of ideal but required if I am to move at all. As I rise to ever more exalted heights, I am greeted rudely by another principle of ladder climbing: the higher one ascends, the greater the reluctance to let go of what is presently in hand in the manifestly vain hope of grasping something else. As one approaches twenty feet, the reluctance to let go at all becomes obsessive. Thus, do I become a stationary object near the top of the ladder, when to my great relief I hear the cheerful voice and see the impish face of Jazz Segien, the proprietor of Northeast Marina. He, it now appears at closer range, is the man with the bald head. With Jazz's encouragement, I gather the will to go over the top.

Jazz and his lifetime friend Ross Furman and some of their friends are sharing jokes over Friday afternoon beers, and they welcome me as though I were an old friend. We are all about the same age and of good humor. Jazz gives me a package of smoked salmon and another of smoked herring that he prepared. His huge, friendly Great Dane joins in the merriment. After a time, I reluctantly bid farewell, and, even more reluctantly, descend the towering ladder, making sure not to look down and asking myself why I didn't just wait for high tide, a mere six or so hours later. From the fuel dock, I relocate *Rascal* behind the fortress-like town breakwater that, by its massiveness, hints at the severity of storms and high seas that must assault it. The pool enclosed by the breakwater is small, so small that the boats within must attach themselves one to another with only the innermost boat attached to the floating dock that in turn is attached to the breakwater. All the boats in the pool are local fishing boats except one very small sailboat, the *Sundowner*, to which I tie up *Rascal*. Its owners, Tony Eager and his wife, Jan, exchange greetings with me and we agree to meet later. By prior arrangement, Ross Furman drives his luxury sedan out to the breakwater to pick me up for a grand tour of Eastport.

Ross is a mildly frenetic entrepreneur. He left Eastport years ago and made his fortune in the vending machine and gaming equipment business. Now, at age fifty-three, he is gripped by the desire to return to his boyhood home, so he travels often from his present home in Portland, Maine, to stay for a few days or weekends at an old, run-down farmhouse he bought overlooking Passamaquoddy Bay. He has renewed childhood friendships and finds that these restore something deep in his soul. We drive to his sister's home. She and a long-time family friend, Aunt Inne ("eye- knee"), are in the living room, where we chat pleasantly. Aunt Inne, I learn, is the Grand Dame of Eastport, having once edited a local newspaper. She happily calls her friend who runs the best B&B in town to reserve me a room for the night. Then Ross and I go out back to the garage, where on the floor sits the largest lobster I could ever imagine, blowing air bubbles and drooling in his last hours of life. He is at least three feet from head to tail, and each pincer is the size of a hubcap. Ross says he has seen such animals easily snap a soft-drink bottle in two. I think what he might do to an arm.

We leave and take the scenic tour around the depressed town of Eastport and the even more depressed nearby Indian settlement. The paper mill that once supplied jobs has now fallen on hard times and may close soon. Aquaculture is a promising employer but does not offer enough new jobs. Buildings are in disrepair. There is a sense of pervasive forlornness. The waterfront tries to be tourist-attractive in the current fashion but falls short. Yet, even here there are as always those few enterprising people who will make a good living no matter the conditions. Jazz Segien is one such. He pumps a lot of fuel from the only floating gas dock for miles around. He sells beer and sundries. He buys and sells real estate. There is also the local guy who gathers lobster and, in off season, takes tourists on his boat to see whales and rare birds. He promotes these tours far and wide. Judging from his packed boat this day, it is a thriving business.

At dinner, I happily join Tony and Jan Eager at their table. He is a tall, slender fellow in his fifties, and she is somewhat younger, demure, and attractive with a sweet disposition. They have chosen as their passion sailing in a tiny sailboat, only twenty-three feet long. Their genius is that they selected a boat small enough to be mounted easily on a trailer and hauled around the country to the many attractive sailing grounds. With their children, they have been doing this for years and now have a shared store of family adventures that binds them together. I have caught Tony and Jan at the end of their first trip alone, he seeming happy to be relieved of family responsibility and she seeming wistful at not having her children around. We say good night and agree to meet at the boats in the morning.

SEVEN

The Bay of Fundy and the Village of Argyle
Eastport, Maine, to Halifax, Nova Scotia

TONY AND JAN warmly greet me at the dock, where I climb over the *Sundowner* to board *Rascal*. We wish each other smooth sailing and fair seas, I cast off and ease *Rascal* out of the protection of the break-water, across Passamaquoddy Bay through Lubec Narrows, and out into the open sea. Once again, the awful fog has descended to blanket our small world. I use the GPS to set an electronic course for the north end of Grand Manan Island some fourteen miles into the ocean from Eastport. Visibility is a half mile. The ocean is icy cold, the coldest I have yet felt. My hands and sockless feet quickly turn red, and I begin to shiver. On reaching the north end of Grand Manan Island, I cannot see its high cliffs hidden in the fog less than a mile away. The fog thickens and I consider laying over at North Head on the island until the fog clears, but dismiss the idea, thinking the fog may never clear. I set a new GPS course for the channel marker at Grand Passage, a channel separating Digby Neck, Nova Scotia, from Brier Island, and set out across the mouth of the Bay of Fundy, cold, utterly alone, and fog bound.

For the first time on this adventure, I am afraid. At forty-five miles an hour, should I hit *anything*—a sea turtle, a floating log, shoal, another boat—only catastrophe could ensue. I could not last more than a half-hour in these frigid waters. All around me there is only cold, grim, menacing water and gray, enclosing fog. My eyes are fixed on the radar display and on what little water I can see ahead. The radar screen is a complete blank. Nothingness and cold water surround me. At such a low temperature, the water is more dense than the semitropical waters far to the south. It feels as though *Rascal* is flying through a sea of oil rather than water. She hurtles over it easily, and when her bow is kicked up by a wave, it settles back cleanly, almost gently.

Suddenly out of nowhere, large waves begin to assault *Rascal's* starboard beam. I guess it must be the wake of a large ship passing nearby, but the successive peaks of the waves are a constant height, not declining as a ship's wake would, and the radar still shows nothing. There is no wind, only stillness and fog. The fear that until now has been my silent companion now leaps to my throat and wholly irrational thoughts assault me. What could be causing this? And then it hits me. Shoals. Somehow, I must have strayed off course and gotten too near the treacherous rocky shoals off the northeast coast of Grand Manan Island. Quickly, I stop *Rascal* and get her position from the GPS, which I locate on the charts. We are right on course, but the course we are on comes too close to the shoals. There is plenty of water below *Rascal*; we are not in danger of running aground. But we are being buffeted by waves from the Bay of Fundy's fast tides as they rip across the relatively shallower water of these extensive shoals. I had not considered this problem in choosing the course. While *Rascal* is tossed about in the open sea, I calculate a corrective course that will take us away from the shoals to a point where we'll take up a new course for Grand Passage. This course will keep us away from the turbulent shoal waters.

The correction made, we set off again as the fog closes in and becomes impenetrable. Visibility is only fifty feet or so. Still, the radar is blank. I stop again to check our course. On the way to Grand Passage, we will pass near more rocky shoals marked by warning buoys. We are close enough that the buoys should show up on radar, but there is nothing. For some reason these buoys are not reflecting the radar's beams. To be safe, I enter in the GPS a correction course out and around these shoals, making sure to avoid them by at least a half mile. With the shoals behind us, we close the last few miles to the channel buoy at Grand Passage, separating Brier Island from Digby Neck. With the GPS, I locate the buoy in the dense fog at a distance of twenty yards. The GPS has done its job. Now I must navigate the few miles through Grand Passage, only a few hundred yards wide, to its exit on the southern end. From there, we will run across open ocean about forty miles south to Yarmouth, on the southwest coast of Nova Scotia. The fog is so heavy we nearly run into the next buoy before I can see it. When we finally exit Grand Passage, the fog is impossibly thick, and still, it is forty miles to Yarmouth. I decide to return to Grand Passage, stay overnight at the village of Westport on Brier Island, and hope for better conditions tomorrow.

We find Westport in the dense fog and are greeted at the town dock by the friendly face of Kenny Graham. He tells me it's okay to tie up against a fishing boat there. He climbs down the long ladder to help me, lugs my bag up the ladder, then takes me in his truck to the Westport Inn, where I get a room, and Kenny and I have lunch. After lunch, he gives me the grand tour of the tiny island, less than three miles long, where he has lived all his life.

During the tourist season, Kenny, his wife, mother, and father operate a large boat for whale- and bird-watching tours. Kenny's father and uncle also own a lobster pound, where they store all the lobster they buy from the local fishermen, then resell them to distributors. The father also raises red deer in a compound near his home. He sells the meat to restaurants and the horn to the Japanese, who grind it up and sell it as an aphrodisiac. I am left to wonder to what extent Japan's population density can be attributed to these industrious Canadians. Kenny works his own lobster boat in season. He has bought a lobster house sitting high on pilings at water's edge, where he makes, repairs, prepares, and baits his four hundred traps with attendant buoys (or pots) and line. Here at Brier Island, lobsters are abundant, but they must be taken at depths that average several hundred feet. They are larger than most lobster and bring top prices. Kenny will net, after expenses, about $60,000 for four months' work. Add that to his share of the profits from the whale-watching boat, and he makes a fine income with very few living expenses. He lives in a modest but comfortable home in Westport, population 375 year-round, and drives a used pickup truck. He will continue to invest his profits in improvements to his boat, in helping his father buy a larger whale tour boat, and in increasing the deer herd. None of this requires that money be borrowed from a bank.

I also meet Clyde Titus, a man of about sixty years with a great shock of wiry white hair. He is a lobster man in season and also catches cod and herring on long lines strung with hook-tipped leaders. The fish he cleans and stores in great vats of brine. When he is not earning income from lobsters, he will collect government unemployment and welfare benefits because technically he then has no income. When lobster season begins and he is no longer eligible for the government benefits, he will sell the salt fish and pocket the proceeds. Clearly, Clyde Titus is a man who has learned how to adapt his business to the circumstances that confront him and to take advantage of opportunities offered by ill-conceived government programs.

~~~

In the first light of morning, I can see the fog has lifted. Blue sky breaks through the clouds. I am elated. After days of fog and gloom, at last, there is sunshine. Eagerly, I cast off the docking lines, gun *Rascal* up to plane, and head out into the open sea for Yarmouth. There are only gentle rollers moving slowly over the surface, and *Rascal* flies over them with ease. Free at last from the grip of the dull gray fog, I am thrilled at the sight of the wide expanse of blue ocean all around me, the sound of *Rascal's* motors roaring happily, the clean smell of the salt air. Not a hint of a problem. Soon we cover the forty miles to Yarmouth Harbor, then set course for the west side of the ominously named Murder Island, where we pick up the narrow, rock-lined Schooner Passage that winds through the beautiful Tusket Islands.

Needing to refuel, I stop and make a cell phone call to the Old

Argyle Lodge in Lower Argyle on Lobster Bay. They are identified in a cruising guide as having gas pumps at the dock. Ginger McKenzie, who with her husband owns the lodge, says they have fuel at the local wharf and, although the pump is closed this Sunday, she'll get the operator to come to the wharf and unlock it. She greets me at the wharf with her husband, Alan Stuart McKenzie, and their three children, Mark, Luke, and Lynn. The pump operator soon shows up too. After refueling, we take Ginger and her kids for a short ride around the nearby islands, avoiding rocks with Ginger's help. On the way back to the dock, with no warning of any kind, misfortune strikes again! The gears of the starboard motor's lower unit freeze up, instantly shutting down the motor. This was the lower unit I had replaced back in Bar Harbor. Fortunately, we have one good motor that gets us back to the dock. At once, Alan and family set about helping me. We arrange to have the boat hauled.

The process of hauling *Rascal* is complicated. Ron Rain's trailer is designed (and built) by him to haul big, beamy lobster boats. *Rascal's* sleek hull doesn't fit very well. As we work at getting her out of the water, I look around and see most of the village's male population lining the wharf. They are fishermen in the off season and word has spread quickly throughout this close-knit community that *Rascal* is here. Her big motors, shiny hull, unusual (by local standards) deck configuration, colorful trim, and racy lines attract admiring stares. Once we get her hauled, Ron delivers the wounded *Rascal* to Paul D'Entremont's Marine Service for repairs.

Alan drives me to their Old Argyle Lodge and books me into a wonderful room with a postcard view of Lobster Bay. Ginger invites me to crew with her and her friend on a twenty-five-foot sailboat in the weekly Sunday afternoon race. Alan's brother, Brian Carmichael McKenzie, lends me his bright red pickup truck for as long as I'll need it. In short, I am befriended by most of Argyle and, because of them, misfortune becomes serendipity.

Alan is a smart, ambitious, active man of about forty years of age. He is a former military operative for the Canadian Army who worked secretively in Central America. Now he is the owner of a private security firm, another firm that inspects fishing boats for the government, and he is the administrator of the mental health units in three area hospitals. He and Ginger own the Lodge, a wonderful building with six rooms upstairs, a restaurant on the ground floor, and a lounge in the basement, sited right on the shoreline of Lobster Bay. It is only a few years old, but it is in a remote location. It seems not to be as profitable as Alan had hoped.

Brian McKenzie is a warm, friendly, athletic man of fifty-four, married to a quiet, kindly wife. They have two sons, who are happily married and have given them three grandchildren. All of the family lives and works in Argyle, as do most of Brian's brothers and sisters. Everyone here seems to be related in one way or another, and their family and personal histories are well known. It is a prosperous community. Brian, for example, works four months of the year as a lobsterman (here called fisherman) and runs four hundred traps that catch forty thousand pounds of lobster and earn him a comfortable living. He chooses not to work in the off season when he hunts, fishes, sails, and enjoys his leisure. I have had the good fortune to break down in Argyle during Brian's off season; we become good friends. He takes me fishing up the gorgeous Argyle River, named for the Hills of Argyle in Scotland. The hills that stand along one bank of the river resemble those in Scotland. We drive to the nearby town of Pubnico to check on the progress of Brian's new boat being built by Lee Goodwin, a strapping, energetic man of about sixty with clear, piercing blue eyes. Lee has the build of a blacksmith and is a skilled craftsman. He built his own home and the two large sheds in which he now builds lobster boats. He is a ship's carpenter, lays fiberglass, installs diesel engines and transmissions, wires boats' electrical systems, everything. He works all the time because he loves it, and there is a backlog of demand for his boats. Brian's boat will cost about $90,000 complete. He will have another $80,000 or so invested in lobster traps and other equipment, a total capital investment of about $ 170,000.

Brian earns a good living and eight months of leisure from his lobstering, but it is extremely hard work and dangerous. He will work six days a week during the season, twelve to fourteen hours a day. The weather will be bitterly cold, some harbors frozen solid. Winds often slam into the coast at more than sixty miles an hour, and frigid seas will pound his boat. Every year, just in the area around Argyle, two or three men are lost at sea, swept overboard by waves, caught in trawl ropes that drag them over, or simply vanish from icy decks. Still, the allure of big profits draws these men from cozy homes and protected harbors into the maelstrom. Once again, I see what a fearsome thing is man's quest for a better life. People will bend themselves to hard labor, they will take monumental risks of personal injury, financial ruin, and even death, all for the hope of improved conditions for themselves and their families.

In a brief period, I have become attached to the tiny village of Argyle. It is like many European communities. All its inhabitants have deep roots here. There are only a few family names, but many families. Most people are born here, go away to the military, to school, perhaps to a job, but nearly all return early in their lives. They join childhood friends who have also returned. They raise families, participate in community affairs, welcome newborns, grieve for the deceased, and pray or not as they see fit. There are athletic competitions. Argyle's people take pride in their prowess in such events as cycling, skiff rowing, badminton, sailing, the always humorous foot races across the local soft mud flats, and the intensely competitive annual lobster boat races. This last event began as a friendly competition among the fishermen using their everyday work boats. In the usual way such things progress, it has become a fierce competition among boats highly customized for the purpose. There now is a special class in which the participating boats have their small, workaday motors removed and, just for the event, have high-performance engines installed. The usually staid, stable, seaworthy lobster boat, when so overpowered, becomes an ungainly water creature that wobbles across the sea at high speeds, remaining upright just long enough to complete the day's races. Then it is returned once again, like Superman to Clark Kent, to its dull, painfully slow plainness, setting out to sea to gather in another day's catch.

Argyle is attractive and functional as European villages often are. There are no billboards, no obnoxious neon signs, no national franchised retail stores, no traffic signals, no convenience stores, no nightclubs or video game parlors. The only stores are a tiny general store, a gas station, and a pharmacy, and these are several miles away. Alan and Ginger McKenzie's lodge is in Argyle, and it has a fine restaurant. There are a few other cafes several miles away. There are no bars at all and little nightlife. All the homes are of the same general architectural style, mostly white with black trim. All are well kept and freshly painted and have flower gardens. Yards are quite large for what are otherwise modest homes. Argyle is not convenient. Most shopping requires a twenty-minute trip into Yarmouth, where there is a K-Mart, a major grocery store, and most other needed stores. The two gas stations are not conveniently located. What Argyle has, far more important than its shops, is a strong sense of community, a shared pride in this tiny place they call home. I feel fortunate to have shared some time here with some of its people.

Rascal is repaired and put back in the water for a test run. I invite Brian and Chris, the young mechanic who made the repairs, to go. She passes the test easily, and I plan to leave early the next morning. That night I bid fond good-byes to all my new friends at the small gathering that follows the Friday afternoon sailboat races and go to bed anxious finally to get back to sea again.

~~~

We leave Argyle early, heading out of Lobster Bay on smooth water, then enter the ocean, which is as smooth as the ocean gets on the North Atlantic coast. I have set the GPS to run a route consisting of fourteen legs from Argyle to Lunenburg. The route will take *Rascal* far out to sea, away from the ledges, rocks, and shoals that lurk just under the surface all along this coast. We round Cape Sable, the southernmost point of Nova Scotia and a notorious shoal area that even on this calm day is kicking up a nasty chop as the currents sweep over it. Just as we get settled in and I begin to enjoy the morning sun rising over the ocean, a fog bank appears out of nowhere. A ghostly curtain lies all across our path a few miles ahead. We have no choice but to enter it. An eerie feeling comes over me as we leave blue sky and sunshine and are instantly enshrouded in this thin, wispy fog. The radar shows nothing. Visibility is no more than fifty feet, so I must rely completely on the GPS. If I made a mistake calculating the coordinates marking the ends of each leg, or entering them into the GPS, we will surely end up on the rocks. Then, just as suddenly as we entered it, we leave this white prison for blue skies. And relief.

As we pass around the south end of Cape Sable, we begin heading north and east, making progress toward the north end of Nova Scotia at Cape Breton Island. There are no other boats, no towns, indeed no sign of human presence at all in sight. We are alone. The wind picks up and, with it, the waves. The ocean surface is an exceedingly complex mosaic, constantly changing, often in unexpected places. Gentle, low rolling undulations, widely spaced, quickly become short, steep moguls as they encounter shallow water. These can become whitecaps as they are blown by the wind or big, nasty waves as they run headlong into opposing currents or tides.

With each turn of the route to Lunenburg, the angle at which *Rascal* attacks the sea changes. As we left Lobster Bay, we headed directly into the prevailing southwest winds. The gentle seas were right on our bow. Then we ran a short leg due south. The winds picked up a bit and the shoals of Cape Sable had their effect, so the waves were higher and coming at *Rascal* on the starboard bow, trying to kick the bow off course to the southeast. The water in the fog bank was dead calm. Now we run a leg dead into steep waves spaced farther apart than *Rascal's* thirty-one-foot length, forcing her to fall from the crest of a wave into the trough behind it, where she lands with a teeth-shattering crash. This leg is run directly into the early rising sun, and its brilliant reflection off the water makes it impossible to see the upcoming waves and prepare for the impact. As we near Lunenburg, conditions change for the better. While the winds have grown to a steady fifteen to twenty miles an hour, the resulting seas are close together and easily handled by *Rascal's* well-designed hull, although the ride is far from comfortable.

The shore along this southeast coast is covered in primeval conifer forest. At the water's edge, the thin soils are weathered away, exposing a wide band of hard, gray, unforgiving rock, in some places a collection of melon-sized stones, in others great boulders, and in still others, solid cliffs or slabs of rock washed by the cold surf. There are no signs of humans anywhere, except the occasional lighthouse. Waterfront development has not yet come to this part of Nova Scotia.

Lunenburg is yet another restored historic town. It is an eighteenth-century British Colonial seaport, brightly painted, perched on a hillside, with all the usual shops and restaurants. The rolling hills and steep rock cliffs around the town's harbor are an attractive framework, dotted by homes perched on hilltops behind. In the center of this framework, the redeveloped waterfront walk winds past actively operating restored machine shops, blacksmith shops, and marine supply stores. Docks all across the waterfront are filled with commercial fishing vessels, lending a presence of commercial life not entirely devoted to tourism.

The pride of Nova Scotia is docked in the harbor at Lunenburg, the old wood schooner *Bluenose II*. Years ago, it was the practice of sailboat captains fishing the productive banks off Nova Scotia and Newfoundland to race their boats against those from other countries. By 1920, these impromptu races became organized and a prize, the International Fisherman's Trophy, was awarded to the winner. It greatly dismayed the proud sailors of Nova Scotia, with its long maritime tradition, that the first trophy was captured by an American schooner, the *Esperanto*. Thus motivated, Angus Walters, a tough captain from Lunenburg, and William Roue, a ship designer, created and built the original *Bluenose*, which won the Cup in 1921 and never lost it. Her last victory was in 1938. After that, she was sold and wound up on the bottom near Haiti, after crashing onto a reef. In 1962, the

Bluenose II, a faithful replica, was built. This is the boat now docked before me on the waterfront.

Leaving Lunenburg, we head out across Mahone Bay and St. Margaret's Bay, popular places for summer cottages, both with an adequate supply of resort towns. I notice the water has warmed considerably from about fifty to about sixty to sixty-five degrees. We are away from the tidal effects of the cold Bay of Fundy, and the warm Gulf Stream is not far offshore. My spirits are lifted as we head on toward Halifax. A nasty chop spawned by the strong winds that have just come up requires some adjustments in the trim tabs and still further adjustments with each course change. We safely round the shoal area guarding the southern approach to Halifax's harbor and make our way into the heart of the city, docking at the public wharves along the waterfront walkway.

As luck would have it, this is a day of the annual Buskers Festival, where a troupe of talented street performers conduct their programs at numerous venues all along the waterfront, some surrounded by standing crowds, others by circular bleachers filled to capacity. The acts include acrobatics, juggling, trickery, foolery, and always humor. The crowds howl with delight late into the night. Each year the festival is a huge success and grows ever larger. Admission is free, in the odd sense that anything supported by a government is free. Some performances are conducted in English, others in French.

The history of more than a few major cities is marred by disaster, sometimes spectacular. San Francisco had its earthquake and fire, Chicago its fire, Atlanta had General Sherman and the Union Army, and, more recently, Miami had Hurricane Andrew. For Halifax, it was a colossal explosion. On December 6, 1917, the harbor was, as usual, filled with ships preparing to sail to Europe with war supplies. That morning, a Belgian ship, *Imo*, collided with a French ship, the *Mont Blanc*, unfortunately loaded with munitions. The resulting explosion wiped out a large part of the city, killed or injured more than 10,000 people, and left 25,000 homeless. The Maritime Museum, just down the boardwalk from where *Rascal* is docked, has a poignant display describing the event that will forever mark the history of this city.

EIGHT

Dramatic Scenery and Terrifying Waves
Halifax, Nova Scotia, to Quebec City

GENERALLY, NOVA SCOTIA'S COAST is sparsely settled. The northeasterly GPS track we take out of Halifax Harbor bound for the Liscomb Lodge runs along coastline virtually devoid of settlement. Seas are running three to five feet with winds out of the southwest. The sky is a gray sheet thrown over the black sea and there is a chill in the haze. *Rascal* is the only boat on the water. With the dark horizon in the distance, no land is visible as we plow ahead, surrounded by bleakness. Some of the GPS legs we run are more than twenty-five miles long. In the rough seas, we can prudently make only about thirty miles an hour, so we must travel nearly an hour to reach the next sea buoy to visually confirm that we are not lost. At last, we reach the buoy offshore of Liscomb and head up the bay to the Lodge, a small government-run resort that has a tiny marina and the all-important gas pump. We have reached forty-five degrees of north latitude. From this point, we are equidistant from the equator and the North Pole. Reaching this point on Nova Scotia's north coast in far southern Canada confirms just how vast is Canada's northern territory.

After refueling and lunch, we leave the calm of the bay, enclosed by forested hills with not the slightest sign of human habitation and confront the sea again. Having learned a few lessons over the past weeks, we resist the temptation to take a tortuous shortcut through rocks and shoals and run about ten miles out of the way to avoid the Canso Ledges. Entering Chedabucto Bay, we are rewarded for our prudence. The sun breaks through and blue sky overwhelms the dreary gray. There are no unmixed blessings, however, and nature charges a price for this relief. Today the price is wind. It rises to more than thirty miles an hour out of the southwest, right on the stern. Whitecaps surround *Rascal* as she gamely slogs her way toward St. Peter's Canal.

At last, we escape the frothy mess of Chedabucto Bay, enter St. Peter's Bay with its tiny canal nestled in the valley of surrounding hills. The village of St. Peter's sits on the hillside overlooking the bay and the canal. As we approach, the scene is European. We could be in France or Austria or the Netherlands as the neatly uniformed attendants open the small lock to admit *Rascal,* close the gates, lower the water level in the lock, and open its exit gates to allow us into the short, winding waterway that leads into the great Bras d'Or Lake. After the turbulent violence of the ocean, the flat, clam water of this magnificent inland lake is a welcome change. We quickly run up West Bay, an arm of the lake, to the Dundee Resort where we stay the night.

~~~

The sky is solid black over the ridge of hills that line West Bay and slope steeply to its shores. Lightning strikes in the distance. High wind and heavy rain descend on the placid surface of the Bras d'Or. Under these conditions, I cannot wisely keep to my plan of rounding the north end of Cape Breton today. The seas outside will be impassable. Instead, we will advance about forty miles across the lakes through the Barra Strait to the resort town of Baddeck, which Jack Burnell and I visited for two days on our car tour of the Cabot Trail. This will put us that much closer to our objective for tomorrow.

The Bras d'Or Lake is well known as among the finest cruising grounds in the world. It is actually a huge system—450 square miles— of adjoining brackish lakes entirely ringed by high wooded hills having a mostly uniform ridgeline. The lakes are deep to the shore, up to nine hundred feet deep. They are generally free of submerged obstructions and offer natural harbors, bays, anchorages, and beaches for the curious to explore. Owing largely to their remoteness and the sparseness of the surrounding population, the Bras d'Or lakes give the appearance of being nearly vacant. The lakes can be entered from the south, as we have done, through the St. Peter's Canal, and can be exited, as we will, through the Narrows, which lead into the ocean along the east coast of Cape Breton. As we make our way across the lakes, we are greeted by extremely high winds that enter the lakes over the hilltops from the ocean and are then tightly funneled by the surrounding hills into a continuous jet of air. A nasty, steep chop is the result, but *Rascal* handles it easily, and we reach Baddeck without incident.

~~~

This is the day I have looked forward to for a long time. It is the day we will make our final voyage in the tempestuous North Atlantic and round the northern end of Nova Scotia along some of the most dramatic scenery anywhere in the world. Once again, it is not a nice day. The front that struck Cape Breton yesterday remains. Skies are gray and the wind is high. Gale warnings are up. As I leave Baddeck and head around the point where Alexander Graham Bell's summer home at Beinn Bhreagh is located, we are greeted rudely by fierce winds blowing from the northeast at, I estimate, as much as forty miles an hour or more. We are in the Narrows, a waterway only about a half-mile wide and lined on both sides with high hills that run parallel to the water. It is in effect a venturi that amplifies the speed of winds whipping in off the North Atlantic twenty miles ahead. *Rascal* confronts the severe, steep waves with ease, but I begin to think it may not be such a good idea to take on the North Atlantic Ocean under these conditions.

As we approach the end of the Narrows, I can look out over the sea ahead. Great waves have built under the driving force of the high winds and are now charging in to dash themselves on the rocky shore. A lump builds in my throat. My grip on the helm tightens. I am filled with anxiety and doubt. The sun, however, has begun to break through the gray clouds, improving my spirits, and I do not want to spend another day and night immobilized by bad weather. It is about seventy miles from the point where the Narrows opens into the ocean to the north end of Cape Breton. There we will turn south along the west coast of the Cape and be in the protected lee of the high cliffs. But it could take more than three hours to get there. Warily, I decide to press on to face the challenging seas.

At first, the waves are very nasty as we head between the mainland and Bird Island. Here the water is relatively shallower than farther out to sea, and the waves pile up steeply and grow closer together as they rush toward shore. They are six to eight feet high, knife-edged, and well defined. To counter them, I take up a course about thirty degrees off the face of the waves. This eases the drop from the peak to the trough and helps *Rascal* to roll over the peak rather than fly over it. Still, it is difficult. I begin to worry, as I watch the waves crest. They may start to break and that would be devastating. If one of these huge waves should break into the boat, *Rascal's* scuppers and bilge pumps would be overwhelmed. She would be quickly slowed and held in place for the next wave, which would undoubtedly swamp her. As I look out to port where the waves that have already struck us are continuing on their way, I can see them breaking in the progressively shallow waters. I have to get to deeper water quickly if we are to avoid catastrophe.

I abandon the course of least discomfort and take a direct line for the deeper ocean, leading directly into the face of the waves. To reduce flying over the peaks and the inevitable violent landing, I have lowered the big trim tabs as far as they will go. The motors are straining under the greatly increased drag, and speed is reduced to no more than about twenty miles an hour. The motors are turning four thousand RPM, a level that in flat water results in more than forty miles an hour. The drag of the trim tabs and the resistance of the seas has cut our speed by half, but the new course begins to pay off. Slowly we get out of the shoal area into deeper water, where the waves change from near breakers to big, rounded rollers spaced farther apart. Because they are spaced too widely, *Rascal* pounds badly as she flies over the tops. Again, I set course thirty degrees off the wind, and this helps.

Now we settle in for the long, rough ride to come, and I can begin to admire the scenery. Running only about a half mile offshore, we pass mile after mile of stunningly beautiful scenery. Sheer rock cliffs plunge fourteen hundred feet straight into the ocean, high rock outcrops intrude into the rough waves as they have for thousands of years. The coastline, as far as the eye can see, stands as a defiant wall, fending off the endless, relentless attacks of the sea. As we reach Cape Smoky, I can see a deep gouge cut into the shoreline like the shape of a human bite. It is cut about two miles deep into the shoreline and is nearly two miles wide and fully exposed to the fierce wind and waves. Its shore is a vertical wall of gray rock reaching up nearly one hundred feet. This is the South Bay of Ingonish. It is separated from the slightly larger but similarly shaped North Bay by a high neck of rock, not more than an average of a few hundred yards across, jutting into the ocean. Perched on top of this neck is the famous Celtic Lodge. At this point, my nerves are strung tight, my mouth is dry, I am filled with apprehension that easily could turn to fear. I need a break, a chance to gather and compose myself. Ingonish seems to be the only possible place for this anywhere nearby.

The chart shows that the bight of South Bay is lined by a solid wall of rock, except for a tiny opening at its far end, a gap in the wall leading to Ingonish Harbor. I decide to change course, enter the bay, and head for this gap. The huge waves that had been on our bow are now giant rollers on our stern, crashing into the bight of South Bay and rushing toward self-destruction against the high cliffs. I raise the trim tabs to free *Rascal's* bow in the following seas. *Rascal* is climbing the backs, then surfing down the steep faces of the waves. At first, I can't see the narrow opening into the harbor. It looks like we are on a high-speed, suicidal collision course, soon to be dashed against the cliffs. Then, as we near the crest of a big roller, and just as I am about to abort the quest for a safe haven, I see the small red floats marking the narrow harbor entry. I can also see that the rollers continue right through the narrow channel and that the channel makes a forty-five-degree turn only about thirty yards beyond its entry. This will be tricky. If we slow, my natural inclination, I am worried that we'll lose steerage. The waves will travel under the boat faster than the boat moves across the water. We'd be like helpless flotsam. I decide to hold our speed, aim for the center of the channel and make a full-speed turn, trying to ignore the effects of the rollers. It works! Thanks to *Rascal's* excellent hull design, she responds well, executing the fast, sharp turn and taking us into the serene waters of this well-protected little harbor. By now, my nerves are shot. I dock the boat and take a peaceful walk a half mile to a local cafe for morning coffee and calmness. I need it.

We leave Ingonish Harbor, passing close by the steep rock cliff where the Celtic Lodge is located. Way up, on top of the cliff, I see several couples, probably from the Lodge, waving to me. I wave back and press on. Not far along the coast, we come to Cape Egmont. At sixty degrees, seventeen minutes of west longitude, our position offshore of the Cape marks the easternmost point of the entire voyage. Just three miles past Cape Egmont we pass magnificent White Point, where Jack Brunell and I had seen the whales, and the breathtaking expanse of Aspy Bay. On the day we saw it, the seas were flat, the skies a warm blue. It was a peaceful place, quite unlike today. Farther along the coast at Cape North, I elect to pass between the mainland and a small offshore island rather than to seaward of the island. The water here is shoal and the waves become steeper and nastier.

BLAM! A loud noise like a gunshot. I feel no impact on *Rascal's* hull, so I know we haven't hit anything. Then I see that the pounding we are taking has sheared off the stainless-steel mounting bracket of the cell phone antenna and it is flailing about on the T-top tethered only by the antenna wire. To repair it, I have to bring *Rascal* to a stop, making sure the transmissions of both motors are securely in neutral. If I fall overboard while working on the repair, it would be a sickening sight to see *Rascal* moving away under her own power, leaving me to certain death. Cautiously, I climb up to stand on the gunwale while holding on securely to the framework of the T-top. Without the motors to drive her forward and hold her bow into the huge waves, *Rascal* begins to drift off, turning her beam to the sea. She begins to roll violently under the force of the waves now hitting her broadside. Using my free hand, I wrap a thin rope several times around the sheared antenna base and force the end of the antenna shaft into a small rubber clamp on top of the T-top. Then I carefully climb down to stand once again on the wildly pitching deck. Working my way around the console, I return to the helm, place the transmissions in gear, and turn her bow back into the seas. I leave her in gear and idle ahead as I leave the helm for the few moments it takes to tie the thin tope tightly around the T-top frame. The broken antenna is now securely lashed down where it can do no damage and may be salvageable.

We are now in the Cabot Strait, separating the south coast of Newfoundland, just over fifty miles to the north, from the north coast of Cape Breton. We continue on and at last round the extreme northwest corner of Cape Breton, another stunning scene called Cape St. Lawrence. Here, we turn and head south along the west coast of Cape Breton, running before the seas. I ease up on the trim tabs, allowing *Rascal's* bow to rise and fall easily as we surf down the backs of the big waves, then climb the face of the next. We pass alongside mammoth granite cliffs, topped by spruce forests. Birds soar across the face of the cliffs. They fly at an altitude only about halfway up the sheer precipices. At places, the cliffs plunge down into great ravines that offer a green-clad opening to the sea, once an ancient river valley. As we move along the coastline, I am awed by the immensity all around me. On one side are these magnificent mountain cliffs and on the other the vast blue expanse of the Gulf of St. Lawrence. Just behind me, still punishing us with the remnants of its turbulent seas, lies the treacherous North Atlantic. In the distance ahead, the cliffs continue for miles as a great wall warding off the fearsome attacks of the sea.

The high waves of the North Atlantic are slowly becoming spent in the calmer water of the Gulf, their size reducing as we move farther to the south, speeding along in the sunshine in one of the great delights of the voyage thus far. We come upon a pod of pilot whales lolling about in the surf, then another pod and another. These shiny creatures, about twice the size of a bottle-nosed dolphin, are all around us. We continue on, mile after magnificent mile. There are no other boats on the now flat, calm blue water as we fly along just offshore, coming at last to the first signs of human life we have seen in hours, the small French Acadian town of Chéticamp. The coastline continues beyond the town as a ribbon of high rocky cliffs, but lower than those we have just passed. The hills leading to the edges of the cliffs are rolling green, some farmland, some forest. Late in the afternoon, we enter the harbor where the Margaree River empties into the Gulf of St. Lawrence and there stay the night in a small B&B.

~~~

The morning brings a reluctant sun, chilled but calm air, and flat seas as we leave the harbor's protective bulwarks and head south, still following the western Cape Breton shore. The jagged cliffs that demark the water's edge continue on, but here they are lower. Their tops now and again are cultivated and more frequently clustered with villages. We leave Cape Breton at Port Hood and take off across the mouth of St. Georges Bay. As we enter the bay, we are hit suddenly by a fierce wind on the port beam, seeming to appear out of nowhere. Looking at the chart, I see that this wind blows in off the North Atlantic Ocean across Chedabucto Bay and is forced into a narrow funnel formed by the Canso Strait and the high hills that line its shores, only to be disgorged in its accelerated fury onto the otherwise calm St. Georges Bay. I am punished one last time by the North Atlantic with this surprise punch. We make it across in the heavy, wet chop to Cape George, marking the eastern end of the Northumberland Strait, separating the mainland of Nova Scotia and New Brunswick from Prince Edward Island, the smallest of Canada's provinces.

We cruise easily along the coast to Pictou, a small harbor town notable as the place where, on September 15, 1773, the first Scottish settlers in Nova Scotia arrived on the ship *Hector*, carrying thirty-three families and twenty-five unmarried men, an assortment that surely led to mischief. A replica of the ship is being built next door to the marina where I refuel *Rascal*. We continue along the south shore of the Northumberland Strait, then, at the point where it narrows, we cross over to the town of Summerside on Prince Edward Island ("P.E.I.", as it's called). On the way, we pass under the skeleton of a monumental bridge being constructed, linking the mainland with P.E.I. At eight miles, it will be the world's longest bridge over water. It is designed to survive the great floes of pack ice that clog these straits in winter.

At Summerside, I find one of the finest marinas I have encountered since Boston. It was built and is owned and maintained by the Summerside Yacht and Curling Club, whose founder and former Commodore I am privileged to meet. He is Dick Wedge, a bearded, cherubic, recently retired pharmacist and still active entrepreneur. He greets me warmly, saying he hopes soon to undertake a trip similar to mine and on a boat just like *Rascal*. Right away I like the man. He has a spirit about him. Without any government help, Dick and his fellow boat enthusiasts built and operate the marina. It immediately became profitable and paid back its cost in just a few years. He shows me around the facility, explaining its details as we go. Some years ago, the Yacht Club teamed with the Curling Club to lower the operating costs of both. A wise move, I thought. There are the expected tensions between participants in the two sports but they are easing over time.

Dick tells me about the winters. In the dead of winter, the ice in the harbor is so thick that Dick routinely drives his truck across the harbor from his home to the Yacht Club and back. To protect the Yacht Club's investment in the harbor facilities, each October all the boats are pulled from the water. At the same time, a crane is hired to lift the floating docks out of the water and stack them up for winter storage, lest they be crushed by the three-foot-thick ice pack that forms inside the harbor. The concrete-filled steel tube pilings, sunk sixteen feet into the harbor bottom, are protected from the ice by an air pressure system. This system sends bubbles constantly flowing up along the outer surface of the piling shafts from the harbor bottom, welling up the warmer water from below, thus preventing ice from closing the last quarter inch around the pilings. If it were not for this, ice would freeze around the pilings, lift them completely out of their foundations, and bend them as if they were toys. Dick and I share stories about family, business, and boats, then reluctantly say good-bye, promising to stay in touch. As we part, I think the town is indeed lucky to have the affection of Dick Wedge.

~~~

Today we face one of the trip's longest open water cruises, from Summerside to Caraquet on the New Brunswick mainland, ninety miles across the Northumberland Strait. The day is cold and gray, but the seas are calm. At least they are calm until we are fully committed, nearly halfway across the Strait. Only then, when we have been lured from the harbor by the promise of fair weather, does Nature renege. The wind picks up to about twenty-five miles an hour, and the waves crash against the starboard bow, sending cold spray to soak me thoroughly. After three unpleasant hours of this, we reach Caraquet, refuel, push on across the Baie de Chaleurs, separating New Brunswick from Quebec, and continue on toward the Gaspé Peninsula. Along the way we come upon the massive, free-standing sheet of rock with a large hole through it, rising out of the floor of the Gulf of St. Lawrence at the tourist town of Percé. The rock is surrounded, as on most summer days, by boatloads of tourists.

We pass the rock and press on to Gaspé Bay and up the quickly narrowing bay to the town of Gaspé. Clinging to the hillsides at the head of the bay, Gaspé could be on a lake anywhere in the French Alps. It is the spot where Jacques Cartier first landed in 1534 and claimed for the French the land that is now Canada. The surrounding hillsides contain homes, the town's commercial area, and forests, all looking down on the small harbor they encircle. Everywhere it looks like Europe: from the architecture to the commercial and public signage, to the tiny cars buzzing about with high-winding motors. We are in Quebec, the insistently French province. In Nova Scotia and New Brunswick, both public and private signs and printed material are in both English and French. Not here. Every visible word is in French only. The effect, along with the other visual cues, is disorienting. We have passed into an altogether different world.

~~~

As we head out of Gaspé Bay along its north shore, we pass by the high rock cliffs that constitute the south wall of the magnificent Gaspé Peninsula. It looks as the coast of Oregon or Washington or Alaska must have looked before civilization took over. We round the even higher, even more dramatic stone faces at the end of the peninsula. These sheer craggy cliffs rise seven hundred feet from the sea and are crowned with juniper forests barely visible through the wispy fog that envelops the cliff tops. We run west about a half mile offshore. This is where the Gulf of St. Lawrence begins to narrow, its northern shore closing ever so gently and unevenly on the south shore, to form the mouth of the St. Lawrence River. Just west of Madeleine-Centre, we pass forty-nine degrees, sixteen minutes of north latitude. This is the northernmost point of our voyage. The water is calm as we pass by miles of high cliffs and one tiny French village after another, each with its Catholic church and prominent steeple. We cover two hundred miles quickly, arriving at our planned overnight stop at Matane by one o'clock in the afternoon. After lunch and refueling, I decide to press on for Rimouski so we'll be that much closer to the Saguenay River and Quebec City.

This proves to be another mistake. Just after we leave Matane, the wind picks up, the seas get nasty, and suddenly there are hundreds of logs floating in the water. The logs are the flotsam from a terrible flood of the Saguenay River a month ago, and hitting one at speed is definitely not recommended. The Coast Guard reports that these will be a problem to navigation for two years or more. To make matters worse, the GPS—the most valued, reliable, and trusted component of my electronic gear—fails. The coastline is visible and provides a useful reference, but there is nothing to tell me where I am along it. The coast is relatively unbroken and free of identifiable landmarks that might help. Although Rimouski is a somewhat larger town than its neighbors, it is unlikely I could distinguish it from the water. The chart shows a long breakwater at the Rimouski harbor that will help identify it, but because of shoal waters and a high concentration of floating logs washed near shore by the currents, I cannot get closer than a mile or more off, too far to see a gray pile of rocks against a dark shoreline. Here my pre-trip planning pays off. I stop, dig out the hand-held backup GPS I brought along, and boot it up. Within a few minutes, I know where we are, precisely.

Just as I think conditions cannot get worse, they do. A heavy fog bank appears out of nowhere. Fog, my nemesis from the upper east coast of the U.S. all the way to the central coast of Nova Scotia. I thought I'd seen the last of it, but it now reappears at a terrible time. Quickly, I turn on the radar. THUNK! A floating log slaps the side of the hull, but because we are at idle speed, it does no damage. It lodges itself against the lower units of the motors. I raise the motors and push it away. The radar shows only the flat, parallel coast, with no breakwater in sight. The GPS tells me to continue southwest, which we do, and in short order, find the high breakwater in the heavy fog. In the dull gray light of a fading day, we enter the safety of the Rimouski harbor, where, in the heavy fog, we stay the night at the city marina.

~~~

At this point on our voyage, we have been gone from home just a few days less than two months. We passed our northernmost point yesterday and are now on the downhill side. From here on, we'll be returning to home port. A hint of regret creeps into my thoughts. I'm not yet ready to be heading home. Maybe I should have gone on to Newfoundland, perhaps Labrador.

We leave Rimouski early under a clear sky with flat water and cool, dry air. We cross the mighty St. Lawrence at an angle to the west, making for the mouth of the Saguenay River on the north shore. It is a wonderful cruise of about fifty miles, the only obstacle being the many floating logs we dodge. As we approach the Saguenay, I spot a gathering of small boats and head their way to see what has their attention. As we near them, I see they are all whale-watching excursion boats circled around pods of huge whales, maybe twenty or thirty of the big mammals. The whales are circling around, porpoising up and down, blowing huge geysers, each blow sounding like a distant, muffled gunshot. We come up to the boats, which have formed a circle about a hundred yards in diameter and turn off the motors to avoid scaring the whales. All the other boats have left their motors at idle. Promptly all the whales come our way, swimming up and down in unison. They are more than twice *Rascal's* size and come so near I can almost reach out and touch their shiny black bodies. I hope they don't take a romantic interest in *Rascal*. They are all around the boat, these gentle giants of the sea, their spray drifting over me, carried by the light breeze. It is an exhilarating moment as they pass by, leaving *Rascal* safely floating in their wake.

After they have dispersed, we head on to the colorful resort town of Tadoussac, sitting on a low hill at the mouth of the Saguenay River. Carefully, I steer a course up the river, eyes fixed ahead to avoid the many floating logs. The Saguenay is really more a fjord than a river. It is lined by high mountains that plunge steeply to its surface and continue to its floor. It is more than seven hundred feet deep in places, like a deep, winding valley in the Rocky Mountains half-filled with water. We wind our way up the river, often no more than a few hundred yards wide, for thirty miles to the topographic marvel that is Eternity Bay. There, a mammoth rock cliff, a half mile across, rises more than five hundred feet straight up from the water surface. I take *Rascal* right up to the cliff wall, being careful not to collide with it.

We reluctantly leave the Saguenay, refuel at Tadoussac, and head up the St. Lawrence along the north shore. Late in the afternoon, we pull into the marina at Isle-aux-Coudres, a resort island at Baie-Saint-Paul. It is a high, tabletop bluff offering spectacular views. The marina, fast alongside the ferry wharf, is well protected, and we dock here for the night.

~~~

The day promises to be a good one—blue skies, not a cloud in sight, a tinge of fall in the air. I am eager to be on the water on such a fine day. At the marina, while preparing to shove off, I notice that even here in the shadows of the high island bluff and behind the big stone breakwater there is a stiff breeze. It is a weather condition, I will later reflect, to which I pay too little attention. When I visit the marina office for a last cup of coffee, the manager in halting English tells me that I shouldn't go out today. Big waves, he says. Very big waves, caused by the wind pushing against the rising tide. He shows me a tide table and says I should wait until late in the afternoon when the flow of the incoming tide will subside. I return to the dock undecided whether to go.

A captain of a sailboat docked near *Rascal* comes over. He explains that the flood tide here is ferocious. It is fed by the ocean currents that push the natural tides against the western end of the Gulf of St. Lawrence. As the Gulf narrows to form the St. Lawrence River, the forces of the currents and the tide together are further magnified by the effect of being pushed into the ever-narrower confines of the river. It is similar to what happens when you put your thumb over most of the opening at the end of a garden hose. The free flow of water from the hose is constricted, and a high-velocity stream results. I am astounded to hear the captain say that the tide is so powerful it completely overwhelms the river's current, reversing the flow of the river back upstream and turning it into a torrent going west at more than five miles an hour. This is the river that drains the entire Great Lakes! I am in disbelief to hear that any force of nature could overwhelm such a current and drive it in the opposite direction at more than five miles an hour. He says that when the tide meets a strong wind head-on, huge, nasty waves develop. These are especially and notoriously bad in the stretch of river from where we are at the Isle-aux-Coudres to the mountain alongside the river called the Sault-au-Cochon (in English, the jumping pig). He does not plan to leave the harbor in his big sailboat and strongly advises me not to go. I look over the charts and see that once in the main channel of the river there are virtually no suitable harbors or protected anchorages along the steep-sided shore for many miles.

Another sailboater comes by and introduces himself as Edouard. He also will not venture out but says that with *Rascal's* speed we could be through the worst of it quickly and that it's really not that bad. If I choose to go, he says he'd like to join me because he needs to get to Quebec City by the afternoon, a sort of subtle encouragement. I decide that I will go, but reason that if it's too rough, I can always turn back. I too am anxious to get to Quebec City. I have total confidence in *Rascal's* seaworthiness in rough water. We survived the St. Andrew Inlet on our first day out, the wrath of the Chesapeake Bay, the remnant seas of Hurricane Bertha, and the harrowing North Atlantic off Cape Breton. If the bad stretch is only the twenty or so miles to the Sault-au-Couchon, we can surely handle that.

And so Edouard and I set out from the quiet harbor into the channel running between the mainland and the island. Immediately I am surprised at the speed of the wind blasting between the mountainous shore and the high island. It is at least gale force, approaching fifty miles an hour, blowing the tops off the white- caps and covering the water surface with white foam. But the waves are modest under the conditions and by lowering the trim tabs to about half their maximum, we take them easily. We exit the island channel and enter the main river about half a mile off the shoreline. Here, in one terrifying instant, we find ourselves confronted by the worst seas I've experienced in thirty years of boating. The waves stand ten feet high. I say "stand" because they are fixed in place by the opposing forces of a five-mile-an-hour current and a fifty-mile-an-hour wind. The waves are almost perfectly vertical and knife-edged. In a near panic, I desperately bring *Rascal* off plane and throttle back to a fast idle.

With each wave, *Rascal* is stood straight up, nearly 90 degrees, it seems. It feels as though she'll be pitched over backward. Then the top edge of the wave passes under *Rascal's* fulcrum, where she balances for an instant before her bow takes a sickening plunge straight down, slamming into the trough with a bone-jarring crash. I wonder how many of these she can take before she begins to come apart. Her stern is held high in the air by the passing wave, and her bow is pointed down sharply in the trough when the next wave is upon us. It hits so quickly and is so steep the bow cannot rise fast enough to float over. The wave breaks over the bow, sending a massive flume of ugly brown water frothing into the cockpit, threatening to sink us. Water swirls around my ankles as the red light on the electrical panel comes on to indicate the automatic bilge pump has come on in response to the invasion. I flip on the switches for the manually controlled pumps as the boat begins to handle sluggishly under the heavy added weight.

Edouard remains calm and that is reassuring to me, but I'm sure he wonders, as do I, why we elected to go. The wind is howling. *Rascal* is taking an awful pounding. I try to attack the terrible waves at twenty-five to thirty degrees off perpendicular instead of head-on, but the slow forward speed of the boat is not enough to counter the force of the water. The waves try to knock us broadside. If they succeed, we'll be instantly rolled over or swamped. We continue ahead, aiming the bow at about ten to fifteen degrees. As the waves slap us off course, I correct with the helm and by applying more power to the port motor. This seems to work.

The relentless assault of these waves begins to take its emotional toll. For the first time, I begin to think we may not survive. If the boat is rolled or swamped or sunk, or if we are washed overboard, we will not last long under the smothering waves. I am in the grip of fear that threatens to turn into panic. I want desperately to be out of this. I remember reading somewhere that in such life-endangering situations to ward off panic you must force yourself to do the simple, mechanical things, to take action in small, incremental steps, to focus on what you know how to do and, in this way, avoid thoughts of your dire condition. I follow this advice, and it seems to work. My adrenaline-charged mind comes under the control of volition as I focus on technique.

I try, crazy as it sounds, to bring *Rascal* up on plane and maybe skip over the top of the closely spaced waves. This is utter desperation.

But the waves make the water far too frothy, and as each wave passes under the stern, the props lose their bite in the aerated water. The motors scream as the props spin wildly, and I yank back on the throttles to avoid blowing the motors apart. The sudden change in the throttle causes the port motor to stop completely. Now, with just one motor holding *Rascal* from being knocked broadside, we are down to our last line of defense. I quickly feather up the throttle on the starboard motor to make sure it does not stall, then restart the port motor. After several more attempts to get on plane, each with the same result, I abandon the idea. It is now one o'clock. We have been at this, fighting to survive, since ten-thirty, two and a half hours that seem like much more, moving ahead at maybe five miles per hour. Still, there is no relief.

Edouard has the idea that we should make for the south shore of the river and hope to pick up some lee protection from the wind. We slowly begin to crab over in that direction, keeping the bow into the waves. Our lateral progress across the river is severely limited by the crushing waves coming at us from directly upriver. If we cross at too much of an angle to the waves, we'll be knocked broadside or swamped by breakers. Between us and the south shore lie numerous small islands interlaced with rock piles and shoals. We have no chart for this area because I had planned to travel the north shore. We edge closer to the rocks. I know if we hit them, we're finished. I worry more about the rocks we cannot see, lurking just below the surface. I reason that in these conditions the hidden rocks will be revealed by a frothy white breaker line at the surface, so we keep a sharp eye out for these. We spot several and navigate around them. At long last, we get near the south shore, but the depth gauge shows that in a short distance the water below us has changed from more than forty feet to less than fifteen, getting shallower quickly as we get nearer the shore. We have achieved some relief from the winds but not enough to risk running aground. We keep far enough offshore to keep at least twenty feet of water under us but get no protection here, and head onward into the still life-threatening waves.

Finally, we get a break. Edouard spots a large ferry boat just entering a breakwater. He recalls there is a marina there. We are both elated that we may yet make it out of this alive. We head for the breakwater barely visible against the gray shoreline and at long last enter its protection. It is a small, modern marina that today is jammed with boats escaping the ferocious seas outside. As we tie up to a dock, a sailboat owner next to us is laughing as he calls out the readings from his wind speed indicator: "Forty-two knots. Thirty-eight knots. Forty knots." This is a speed of almost fifty miles an hour. I am overcome with the elation that I suppose must come to a man on death row whose sentence is commuted after he has been strapped into the electric chair. It is combined with utter exhaustion of mind and body. It is two o'clock. Every fiber of my being, physical, intellectual, emotional, has been intensely focused on survival for the past three and a half hours, and the sense of relief from this struggle is overwhelming. After we secure the boat, Edouard's wife comes to drive us into Quebec City, taking me to my hotel. I will retrieve *Rascal,* still some twenty miles from the city, tomorrow. Or maybe later. Right now, I need a drink.

Now safely on land, with my mind at rest after the strains of survival, I reflect on how I got myself into today's near disaster. The simple, and perhaps accurate, answer is that I unwisely chose to ignore adequate warning about what lay ahead. But, put into context, it was not so foolhardy a decision. With each violent sea we have faced and survived has come an ever-growing confidence in *Rascal's* seaworthiness and my own skills. I have come to believe that there is almost nothing, short of a hurricane, that we could not survive. We have faced seas that were extremely rough, huge waves that intimidated, endless hours in extreme discomfort, the lonely desolation of cold fog over black water. We have traveled many miles in such conditions, sometimes with my life seemingly in imminent danger. Therefore, the warnings issued to me by the marina manager, put into this context, were not so dire. And Edouard, an experienced boater in these waters, volunteered to go with me. I took that as an expression of confidence and gave it greater weight than the warnings of the marina manager.

If I erred, it was in not identifying how serious the conditions were before it was too late to turn back. It all happened so suddenly that I'm not at all sure this was possible. One minute we were in the choppy but tolerable water in the channel adjacent to the island, shielded partly by the mountains, and the next we faced the monster waves. Yes, more cautious souls would have heeded the warnings, opted for the comfort of the marina, waited overnight for the winds to subside, and enjoyed a fine, gentle cruise into Quebec City the next day. Clearly, I am not cautious by nature and have often paid a price for the lack of it, but that is how I am constituted, how I have chosen to live, and I harbor no regrets about it. Today's events were part of the risks assumed by a person of my constitution undertaking an adventure in an outboard boat on foreign waters. In the final analysis, I conclude this was just one of those things that can happen for which there is very little to be done except to give my best once into it.

Many years ago at the Indianapolis 500 race, as the cars finished their pace lap and accelerated down the front straightaway for the green flag, a terrible accident occurred involving perhaps a dozen cars. One of the drivers involved was A. J. Foyt, then at the peak of this career. His car emerged from the fiery core of the crash, spinning wildly. After several hundred yards of 360-degree loops down the front straight, he crashed unhurt into the inside guard rail. Later he was asked, "What do you do when a crash like that happens?" He replied, "You drive the car till it stops." Somehow, this day, with its life-threatening peril reminded me of A.J.'s philosophy of driving.

NINE

A Great City and Great Lakes
Quebec City to Chicago

I HAVE TAKEN A ROOM IN OLD QUEBEC at the huge, venerable Château Frontenac, magnificently sited at the top of the high, steep cliffs on which the old city lives. These very cliffs on which I now stroll played a crucial role in Canada's history, a role still appreciated by her citizens and commemorated in the monuments dotting the landscape. It was here that the most important battle in Canada's history and perhaps the most important in the Seven Years War between France and Britain was fought. A theater of that war, declared in June 1756, promptly opened in America, where both sides saw the future importance of the vast territories. France reinforced its detachments, then under the command of the Marquis de Montcalm. Britain, whose forces were commanded first by Juben Loudon and later by James Wolfe, did the same. The British forces were significantly stronger in numbers, with ten battalions, superior fire power with both field and siege artillery, and naval support with thirty-eight warships. Montcalm managed early victories by capturing Fort William Henry, then defeating a British attack led by General Abercromby at Fort Carillon, inflicting heavy losses in the process. The British then won successive engagements, first at Fort Frontenac at present-day Kingston on Lake Ontario, then at Fort Duquesne on the Ohio River. The French then suffered a major loss when the British captured their important fort at Louisbourg on the east shore of Cape Breton Island in Nova Scotia.

After Louisbourg, the British turned their attention to the place where I now stand at Quebec. They were commanded by Wolfe and numbered about nine thousand soldiers, supported by a battle fleet of forty-nine warships. They faced Montcalm and nearly fifteen thousand men. Wolfe's problem was how to get at the French, occupying a strong fortress high on top of these sheer cliffs, protected by batteries of artillery. The problem was solved when Wolfe himself selected a place on the cliffside, l'Anse du Foulon, where his army could ascend, then personally led the assault that sent defenders fleeing. Wolfe's forces scaled the heights and formed into lines of battle. Montcalm, using doubtful judgment, left the protection of his fortress and formed his army on the famous Plains of Abraham, now a fine memorial park. The French governor refused to allow Montcalm to commit a significant number of the available garrison to this strategy, leaving Montcalm outnumbered. It was over in twenty minutes. A single volley of British muskets routed the French, who retreated to their fortress. Both Wolfe and Montcalm received fatal wounds and are memorialized within a stone's throw of my hotel. There were a few more engagements after Quebec, but essentially it was over. The modern history of Canada had been cast.

Quebec is a fabulous city. It comes closer in its old section to urban perfection than any place I know. Its scale is human. There are no great, glistening glass towers expressing man's triumph over natural forces, only stone buildings, most of two or three floors, resolutely French European in style. At street level, they hold inviting cafes, many of them open-air, bistros, quiet bars, shops, all with thematically consistent but not rigorously structured storefronts and signage. It is not cute, as so many restored historic towns seem to be. There is individual expression, though tasteful and muted. Streets, as always in old towns, are narrow, but in Quebec, for reasons I could never apprehend, they are not clogged with noisy traffic. They are welcoming to the pedestrian, easily strolled upon. If cities are to be anything more than an agglomeration of vertical office parks, it is essential that they have a thriving residential component, and Quebec does. In fine, old restored buildings, above street-level stores, in blocks of low- to mid-rise modern but tasteful and harmonizing apartments, people go about the routines of living out their lives, happily intermingled with the hubbub of an active tourist trade and a profusion of commercial shops.

There are splendid, manicured, tree-covered, flower-festooned parks. Hills, steep ones, that curve and wind down to rivers edge, crossed by stairways going this way and that, provide topographical variety. A city marina, right in the heart of town, is entered only through a lock that lifts boats into the protection of a bulkheaded harbor. Everywhere a visitor could want to go is an easy and generally interesting walk away. And then there is the fabulous Château Frontenac. If one building can represent the soul of a city, this is it for Quebec. It completely dominates the skyline, perched high on the same cliffs that Montcalm rode along as he surveyed the vast force assembled on the St. Lawrence River below him. Along its promenade, people stroll, gazing down the beautiful St. Lawrence at the Île d'Orléans, and the north and south channels that surround it. There is little crime. People walk the streets at all hours of the night without the least fear of attack. The place is spotless, swept regularly, and though its buildings are old, they are lovingly maintained. It is a thoroughly French city, the provincial capital of Quebec. One supposes, for these reasons, that Quebec is a monument of sorts and thus the beneficiary of considerable government support. Whatever the reason, it is a place to which I will return, and soon.

~~~

Regrettably, after three marvelous days, we must leave this enchanting city. The day after the wind storm passed and the waves subsided, I moved *Rascal* the few miles upriver to the Port of Quebec marina, from which we now depart, bound for Montreal. The trip is uneventful if choppy, even rough. The word "Quebec" comes from the Indian word "Kebec," meaning place where the waters narrow, and narrow they do. From the broad, mountain-lined expanse at the Gaspé Peninsula, the river gradually narrows, dividing in two at the Île d'Orléans, rejoining at the city to form a wide bay. It then narrows quickly along the cliffs scaled by Wolfe and his soldiers. Farther west, the river becomes wide again, but surprisingly shallow outside of the marked channel. Both shores are dotted with tiny villages, one after another. These are timeless, quiet places on low, gently rolling plains. Behind them, forming a serene backdrop, are carefully tended rows of small farms.

We pass great ships, freighters, and tankers, steaming this nautical highway of commerce. When running at their maximum allowed speed for the river, some generate enormous wakes. *Rascal*, with trim tabs locked down tightly, handles these waters easily, but I saw a fifty-foot sailboat take a wake on its stern and nearly roll over. These maritime giants are the gorillas of the river, and pleasure craft cruise with them uneasily. After about 160 miles, we arrive at Montreal, where I arrange to have *Rascal* hauled and delivered to a marine service center for repairs and routine maintenance. Here, I have the broken cell-phone antenna fixed along with the all-important GPS. David St. Laurent, the man I met with his girlfriend in Martha's Vineyard, is a native of Montreal, fluent in French, and an invaluable help in making these arrangements.

Montreal is a city of more than two million people, mostly French speaking, called Francophones, a minority of English speaking, called Anglophones, and a mixture of other immigrants, called Allophones. It sits on an island in the river at the head of the Lachine Rapids and was in its earliest years the site of a portage around them. Today the St. Lawrence Seaway and its system of mammoth locks circumvent these and the other rapids upstream. Montreal today is a city of mixed cultures, with French dominating. It is big, noisy, congested, and dirty. Sitting imposingly near its center is Mount Royal, whence the city's name, now a huge park.

Were George Orwell alive today, he would say, upon visiting Montreal, "See, I told you so." He would say this when he discovered the Language Police. This is the street name for the Quebec Provincial government agency, armed with broad police powers, charged with enforcing Quebec's language laws. While I was in the city, a group of dutiful functionaries from this agency raided a popular old restaurant during its busy lunchtime. They forcefully removed from the place some signs they deemed in violation of the language law. This was done without prior warning or notice, without asking the owner to please change the signs, and, needless to say, without a prior court order. The offending signs, it turned out, were in both French and English but, for shame, the print of both languages was of equal size. The law requires that the French letters appear on top and be twice as large as the English! The aggressively French-speaking people of Quebec and the mostly English-speaking people of the rest of Canada may one day resolve their differences and live in harmony as one country. But I am not optimistic.

To pass around the Lachine Rapids is to advance in one step from 1957, the year the St. Lawrence Seaway was completed, to the present. Prior to that year, the rapids and others along the river were an impassable obstruction to commercial navigation. The seaway is a triumph of modern engineering. It begins, this victory tour, at the St. Lambert Lock in Montreal. There, *Rascal* and I present ourselves to the lockmaster, along with a dozen or so other pleasure craft, to be raised about thirty feet, then set free to proceed upstream. It is all a transparently simple process. You can watch what the many local boat owners do and emulate them or follow the written directions in the several commercially published cruising guides or in the official— but not very helpful—guide for small boats. As a last resort, you can just follow your instincts.

There are seven locks on the seaway: the St. Lambert, the St. Catherine, the two at Beauharnois, the Snell, the Eisenhower, and the Iroquois. Each of the locks, except the last, lifts westbound boats what looks to be about twenty-five feet, for a total of about 150 feet. This will vary somewhat depending on rainfall, snow runoff, hydro-electric requirements, and other considerations. The St. Lawrence

Seaway Development Corporation, a joint venture of the U.S. and Canadian governments, operates the waterway to maintain a controlling depth that will allow the big ships to carry a maximum load without grounding. When the required depth cannot be maintained for whatever reason, the ships must lighten their cargo loads with a resulting loss of revenue. Ships that use the Seaway are built with a beam that is barely narrower than the locks. When the ships enter a lock, they often use a technique whereby they intentionally place the bow hard against the massive concrete walls that extend outward from the lock itself and move forward, sliding the bow along the wall to guide the ship into the lock. Most of the ships I saw had harsh scrape marks along the length of their freeboard, indicating they had been "sliding the wall." Watching one of these ships disgorge itself from a lock is vaguely reminiscent of watching childbirth.

After bypassing the Lachine Rapids with the St. Lambert Lock, we attempt to bypass the Split Rock, Cedar, and Coteau Rapids with the two Beauharnois Locks. The lockmasters are required to give priority to commercial ship traffic. Pleasure craft can enter a lock only when there are no commercial vessels needing to go through. If it is late in the afternoon and there is a line of ships awaiting passage, a small boat is stuck for the night. So it is for *Rascal* and me at the lower Beauharnois Lock, where a man who introduces himself as Guy was also waiting with his wife on their boat. When it is obvious we would not get through by dark, Guy invites me to dock at his home marina just next to the lock. The marina owner and manager, Homer, comes out to greet me, then drives me to a nearby inn, where he introduces me to the inn's owner, his good friend, Denis. Denis's wife prepares a wonderful French meal for me. The next morning, we leave early with Homer and Guy on their boats and at least a dozen other pleasure boats in a holiday flotilla that moves cheerfully through both Beauharnois Locks. When there are so many small boats, the lockmaster requires that the larger ones secure themselves to one of the lock's walls with tended lines provided by the lock attendants. Smaller boats then raft against the larger ones. On this Labor Day weekend

(Canada has one too, on the same day), the groups of rafted boats are full of merriment as their captains and crews head off to holiday fun.

Safely through these locks, we pass through choppy Lake St. Francis and stop on the U.S. side of the river for lunch. There I meet David, a tall, skinny boy in his early twenties. He describes himself as a half-breed Iroquois and tells me the place I have chosen to stop is an Iroquois Indian Reservation and a hotbed of smuggling. Interested, I encourage him to say more. According to his account, the Indians, because they are on a reservation that is, in essence, a tax-free zone, can buy liquor and cigarettes in the U.S., free of the high U.S. sin taxes. This they do in massive quantities, buying from sellers in those states that also have low state taxes on the products. They then smuggle their cheaply bought bounty into Canada, where taxes are outrageously high, and sell it for a handsome profit. Economists call this "arbitrage," buying goods in a low-price market and selling the same goods in a high-price market. The highly socialized Canadian government is getting a painful lesson in free-market economics from the entrepreneurial, if mildly larcenous, Iroquois Indians. I then notice that he has a very fast, small boat painted black, with a large open deck ideal for carrying cargo. I ask if he is a smuggler and he readily admits he is. He says most of the young men on the reservation are also smugglers because the money is good and there are no other jobs. He is often chased by the cops (I presume Canadian tax authorities or Coast Guard) and has been shot at.

He admires *Rascal*, then delivers a warning so sincerely that I heed it: "They won't steal your boat. Too fancy. Cops would spot it too easy."

"That's comforting," I reply, growing uneasy now that the conversation is becoming focused in my direction.

"But they'll get your big motors. Steal them in the middle of the night. Cut your throat and throw you overboard if you're in the way. Won't think twice about it," he says. "You're safe so long as it's daylight. They won't hit you now. But you better be long gone by dark."

He delivers this warning in a cool, matter-of-fact tone. He's not joking. "Look," he continues, "I don't owe you a thing, but you seem like a nice guy, and I like your boat. I don't want to see you get hurt. Just take my advice. These Indians around here are tough, and they'll get you."

We have in just a few minutes changed the tone of conversation from casual friendliness to chilling threat. I begin to look around the area warily, now concerned that despite David's assurances we might be at risk. It looks innocent enough, but his warning is given so coldly, without a hint of bravado, that I decide to leave immediately. I thank him for his advice, cast off, and head out into the river. My natural incautiousness with weather and sea conditions does not extend to potential confrontations with Indian engine pirates. We pass on to the last lock in the seaway, fittingly, the Iroquois. There is so little lift here that a sluiceway adjacent to the lock is wide open. *Rascal* just barely slides under an open sluice gate, and we're off again, making for the Canadian town of Prescott, Ontario.

We have entered the Land of Eh, pronounced here as a long *a*. "Eh" is a linguistic filler expression, similar to but easier on the ear than "you know," and it is heard everywhere in Canada but especially in Ontario: "A bit cool today, eh." It seems to be heard only at the end of sentences, turning each into a pop quiz. It is as though the speaker wants to be sure you're paying attention and so queries you with almost every sentence. It has the advantage of economy over its U.S. counterpart, but to my ears, it is used more frequently, perhaps because it is briefer.

~~~

The Thousand Islands (whence comes the name of the salad dressing, the recipe for which originated in a restaurant here) lie at the area where the St. Lawrence River begins its journey to the sea, in the northeast corner of Lake Ontario. A chart of these islands looks like a house painter's well-used drop cloth, a broad, consistent background with intermixed patches of irregular shape and varied size. The islands are smooth rounded heads, slabs, and mounds of gray granite rising from the surrounding blue waters, crested by conifers, hardwoods, and, in modern times, by homes, cabins, and a few castles. They are closely clustered in groups—such as the Brock Group, the Admiralty Islands, the Navy Islands, and the Summerland Group—and the groups are themselves clustered, forming a complex tapestry through all of which the river flows. This is an enchanting place. No wonder it's so crowded on this Labor Day weekend. The waters are filled with sailboats, ski boats, skiffs, runabouts, small cabin cruisers, sport boats, and, of course, the abrasively loud high-performance ocean racing boats brought to these calm waters for hormonal exhibition. We visit Alexandria Bay on the U.S. side. It is an impossibly crowded, tacky tourist place filled with hundreds of small boats dodging each other in the harbor.

We leave Alexandria Bay and head for Kingston, Ontario, a pleasant, well-kept town with a handsome waterfront graced at its center by the City Hall. Jutting assertively out into Lake Ontario is a peninsula nearly covered by the ramparts of Fort Henry, looking as if it were brand new. Sitting between the fort and the city on another peninsula is the European-looking compound of the Royal Military College and adjacent Fort Frederick. The city today is alive with Labor Day tourists wandering about the waterfront and strolling around the manicured gardens of the City Hall. I decide to avoid the crowds and spend this night as my first night of the voyage onboard *Rascal,* so we head back to the Thousand Islands, where we find tiny, charming, and uninhabited Camelot Island, just off the northeast corner of the very large Howe Island. The obvious anchorages are filled with sailboats and power cruisers layed up for the night, so we choose a spot open to the channel but also to the prevailing light breeze and a view of the sunset. After the noisemakers in the high-performance boats go home for the night, the water surface becomes mirror flat, then turns to burnt orange as it reflects the setting sun. Darkness settles in and the sky glitters with starlight as I turn in for the night.

~~~

We get an early start and head back toward Kingston, then into the protected, deep waterway of Adolphus Reach, leading into the famed sailing grounds of the Bay of Quinte. Shaped like a Z and less than a mile wide in most places, it is lined by high wooded hills that concentrate and intensify wind forces. Today, however, the bay is flat and calm, the color of pea soup. We stop for refueling at a fine marina in Belleville, then head on, passing through the Murray Canal, where the toll is paid by stuffing the money in a tin cup at the end of a long pole extended by the attendant, through Presqu'ile Bay into the green waters of Lake Ontario. We continue about twenty-five miles along the shore to Cobourg, another charming, spotless little town gracing the north shore of the lake just east of Toronto.

~~~

To get from Lake Ontario into the Georgian Bay, located along the northern reaches of Lake Huron, there are two choices. The first is to take the Trent-Severn Waterway. This scenic route begins at Trenton, on the north shore of Lake Ontario, and twists and winds its way up over hills and back down to Port Severn on the southeast end of Georgian Bay. It has one significant deficiency of which I was aware when I planned this voyage. In order to get a waterway to go up and back down a hill, a system of locks is required. These raise the waterway in increments by clamming one side of the lock at a higher level than the other side and lifting boats from the lower to the higher level. The lifting in most locks is done by admitting boats into the lock chamber from the low side, closing the lock gates behind them, flooding the chamber with water taken from the high side until the level in the chamber is just equal to that at the high side, then opening the gate to discharge the boats onto the higher water level. It works the same way in reverse when going from higher to lower water. The Trent-Severn has forty-four of these locks along a horizontal distance of 240 miles. The process for locking through can require considerable time. From the time a boat requests to be locked through, to the time it is discharged on the other end, can easily consume thirty minutes to an hour, more if the lock gates have just closed ahead of you and you must wait for the completion of the entire cycle. *Rascal* can ordinarily travel 240 miles on an easy day. The Trent-Severn—with its locks and its many slow-speed zones through the many small villages—would take about four days to navigate, depending on lock operations. This is the route I had originally planned to take.

The other choice is to have the boat hauled out of the water, placed on a trailer, and driven to a port on the Georgian Bay. The process takes about three hours. At this point, the choice between four slow days of locks and no-wake zones versus three hours by land seems easy. I choose the tractor-trailer, and this is how I came to know Ed Pursey. By prearrangement, I meet Ed at the Cobourg City Marina on a beautiful, sunny day. He drives up in a huge, sparkling gray truck tractor pulling a semitrailer specially designed for hauling boats of all shapes and sizes. The truck glistens in the sun, its chrome wheels and exhaust stack nearly blinding. On the side of the truck cab, neatly printed in bright red, are the words "Pursey's Yacht Portage, Ltd., You Call, We Haul, That's All.' After backing the trailer onto the boat ramp, Ed stops the big rig and jumps out.

The first thing I notice about Ed is his energy. Though in his sixties, he moves quickly, with a spring in his gait. He is not a tall man, but he is muscular and trim. His burr-cut hair is pure white, not long enough to be called a flattop. It is only slightly longer than his full, neatly trimmed beard. His square jaw and direct manner give him the look of a retired Marine drill sergeant. The similarity continues when he talks. Ed has the loudest voice in ordinary conversation I have ever heard. He seems to shout each word, and each is infused with his energy and good humor. His bright blue eyes sparkle and he grins impishly as he talks. Ed, like a number of the people I have encountered in Canada, is engaging and picturesque. He dons a full-length canvas apron to protect his clean shirt and jeans.

Together we easily load *Rascal* onto his trailer, I climb into the high, plushly-appointed truck cab, and we head out for the town of Midland, Ontario, on Georgian Bay. Ed never cared much for school. "Hated every day of it," he booms in his friendly way. He quit after the sixth grade. Before he was of age, he tried to join the Canadian Navy, but they caught him and he joined the Army instead. After he got out, he went back home to Cobourg. His father, whom Ed admired greatly, had worked all his life as an employee of an oil company in a service station. He fixed flats, repaired motors, pumped gas—and he taught Ed. When Ed went back home, he bought the service station from the oil company and set about building a business of his own. He worked as his father had done, but now he was his own boss. He took good care of his customers and they were loyal to him. The business grew and he prospered. He made a good living, raised two daughters, then decided to retire. The oil company leased the station from Ed for a fifteen-year term, giving Ed a comfortable pension. But instead of sailing off into the sunset—he's an avid boater—Ed had to keep busy, so he started hauling boats for friends, then others, and four years later he has more business than he can handle—including me, another satisfied customer.

~~~

The Georgian Bay and the adjoining North Channel combine to form a large branch of Lake Huron. They are separated from the main body of the lake by a peninsula and a chain of islands. On a nautical chart, the north shoreline of Georgian Bay resembles nothing so much as magnified Velcro. I don't know of another shoreline like it. They call it the Thirty Thousand Islands, but that seems to be an undercount. To call its waterways tortuous would be irresponsible understatement. I am thankful that the channels through it are well marked with red and green buoys and that the charts for it, like all Canadian charts, are excellent. We leave Midland harbor early in the morning and begin to thread our way through this complex maze. The islands are all low rock outcroppings, intricately formed, complex, and wildly irregular. Most are topped by hardy stands of conifers stunted by the harsh winters and the thin little rocky soil. We twist, wind, dodge rocks, thread narrow gaps, change course, slow down, speed up. Often, we change course so sharply we head in the direction from which we just came. Closer to the towns along the eastern shore, most of the larger islands support a cabin. These are modest, rustic affairs, and after Labor Day, are mostly vacant. Farther west, the islands are wild, empty, and primitive.

We stop at Snug Harbor, where I talk with Don. He is one of the few who live here year-round. He says the water freezes out into the big lake, and snowmobiles are the only means of supply. When winter storms come, as they always do, and the temperature drops far below zero, one must be in a well-heated cabin or on a snowmobile. The cabin I understand, but a snowmobile? Don explains that snowmobiles have hand warmers that work off the battery, and to operate them you must wear a snowmobile suit. With these, you can survive almost anything. The grave danger is that you venture onto thin ice and fall through. That's why the trails are marked, to keep travelers over the thick ice or land. There are hundreds of miles of trails. Each winter, as the water ices over, a team of men works its way along the trails, drilling auger holes into the ice to test its thickness. Where it will support man and machine, a tall stake is placed to serve as a road marker. As long as a snowmobiler stays within the marked paths, he is safe. Last winter, Don put 3500 miles on his "sled," as he calls it, running errands, visiting friends, shopping in the nearby towns, and ice fishing.

From Snug Harbor, the channel leads out to sea through a bad shoal area. Don helps me plot a course through it all and tells me what to watch for. *Rascal* and I push off. The channel winds its way back into the dense Velcro patch of islands and rocks. We turn, twist, and wind some more until once again the channel leads into the broad, open waters of the bay and on toward our destination. Then the channel markers lead us around a cluster of rocky islets called The Chickens, through Beaverstone Bay, and into a unique passage, called the Collins Inlet. Not more than thirty yards wide at one place, it is a long, fairly straight stretch of deep water lined on both banks by high rocky cliffs. The visual effect is of being in a rock-walled corridor. We continue on, in a westerly direction, through the cliff walls and the remote, magnificent Killarney Provincial Park until at last, we reach

Killarney Channel, lying between the mainland and George Island. The channel is used as the harbor for the village of Killarney, where we stay the night in the rustic Killarney Mountain Lodge, built in the late 1940s by the Fruehauf Trailer Company as a private retreat. Roy Fruehauf and Jimmy Hoffa, also in the transportation business, in a way, were great pals. Hoffa frequented the lodge. Legend has it that Hoffa completed some of his infamous deals on the premises. The lodge was sold to its present owners in the 1960s who opened its charming forty-six rooms to the public.

~~~

I thought we surely had seen the last of fog, our old adversary, but here it is again. Visibility is only a few hundred feet as we set out for the passage between Georgian Bay and the North Channel of Lake Huron. With radar, GPS, and the charts, we make slow, careful progress, one channel marker at a time through the eerie, dense fog. We are surrounded by mountains, rocks, and islands, so many that the radar screen is a hopeless jumble. I cannot distinguish channel markers from rocks except by also locating them on the charts and comparing the chart with the radar screen. Even then I creep along toward each marker, uncertain that we are heading in the right direction. After two hours of this, we, at last, reach the village of Little Current, lying alongside the channel between Great La Cloche Island and Manitoulin Island, where, as if by magic, blue sky appears. Grateful for the relief, I promptly head out into Clapperton Channel, round the north end of Clapperton Island, and into McBean Channel. We are in more open water now. The islands are much larger and more widely spaced except for the occasional narrow channel. The day turns out to be beautiful, even a bit warm, as we cruise through these high, rocky islands. There is not another boat or person in sight. This is dazzling, stunningly beautiful country.

Regretfully, we pass out of the groups of islands into the calm, blue-green waters of the North Channel and head due west along latitude forty-six degrees, six minutes. *Rascal* is running well, flying along easily over the cool, fresh waters. I savor this time, luxuriating in the warm rays of the sun I have lately felt too seldom, awed by the beauty of the wide, blue waters all around. It is over in a few hours. Near the west end of the North Channel is the shoreline of Drummond Point, Michigan, and just around the Point is the lower end of the St. Mary's River, which connects the North Channel and Lake Huron with Lake Superior. I am reminded how far we are from the first St. Mary's River we crossed our first day out of Jacksonville. We head for Detour Passage, a narrow, short waterway where the St. Mary's joins the main body of Lake Huron. As we near the Passage, I see five huge ships in the area, moving up and down the St. Mary's. I also see fog. In the distance, several miles away, lying completely across our track and sitting right on top of Detour Passage is a heavy blanket of fog. There are blue skies everywhere else. It is as though Mother Nature has erected a barrier to prevent *Rascal* from getting through the Passage. But get through we must, if only to reach the marina inside the Passage to refuel.

As we approach the fog bank, I steer a course for the far side of the Passage, where we will run along the shoreline far enough off to avoid obstacles in the water but close enough to avoid the ships, who will not stray as close to the shore as we can. I reduce speed to fast idle, turn on the radar, and watch it carefully. I cross-check my position constantly, using the GPS, radar, and the chart for the Passage. I locate first one, then another, and another of the channel markers, nearly hitting them before I spot them visually, so thick is the fog. After finding the marker that the chart shows is directly off-shore of the marina, and cross-checking our position on the chart, I turn and take a compass course for the spot where the breakwater for the marina should be, and at last, looming out of the gray fog, the marina appears.

It is early in the afternoon, and I must decide whether to stay here for the night or continue on to the original destination of Mackinac Island. If the fog is like this all the way to Mackinac, I couldn't get there by nightfall traveling at low speed, so the question is whether this is a large blanket extending all thirty-three miles to Mackinac or just a local patch hanging over the Passage. The people in the marina don't know. I call the marina at Mackinac and they have seen no fog all day. It's clear and sunny there. I conclude that the fog is a local patch concentrated over the Passage, probably brought on by lower water temperatures in the turbulent Passage itself. I decide to move on. Slowly, we move out of the marina and on the radar promptly spot a big ship moving through the Passage. He sounds his foghorn. I stick to the bank, watching the depth gauge to be sure I don't get too shallow and the chart to avoid obstructions. The ship passes safely, and I easily locate and visually identify the first two channel markers. The next one should be easy as well. It is a mammoth fog signal standing seventy-four feet above the water on a huge platform. This will be my departure point for the route to Mackinac Island.

On the radar screen, I see the image of a large object that must be the fog signal and head toward it, hearing its intermittent bleating. And then it happens. As I stare through the fog ahead, precisely where the fog signal tower should be, suddenly I see a huge ship bearing down on me not more than a hundred feet away! My heart jumps to my throat. I'll be crushed under its looming prow for sure. In an instant, my right hand grabs desperately for the throttles, and my left lunges for the helm. Too late. *Much* too late. We'll be smashed any second. An instant later I realize the ship is only the big fog signal sitting there passively. A wave of relief comes over me, as though I have been snatched from the jaws of death. I laugh at myself out loud and sit down to recover my composure. How stupid of me. But at first glance in the gray fog, the thing looks like a ship's bow. An excusable mistake. Thank God it wasn't the real thing. What an awful scare!

Then, as if to balance the good with the bad, blue sky appears just past the fog signal. It's not exactly in the direction I want to go, but it's out there and that means this fog is only a patch. I gun *Rascal* up on plane and head out for the blue sky. It opens up still more until in a short while *Rascal* is flying across the calm, blue water of Lake Huron, seeming glad to leave the fog of Detour Passage behind. As I look back, I can see the thick cloud sitting there with clear sky all around.

We make the thirty-three-mile run to Mackinac's harbor using the GPS to fix the exact destination and course. Once we are settled in on the proper course, I set the autopilot to hold that course and kick back to enjoy the day. We arrive in less than an hour at a fine harbor set behind two long breakwaters and find a slip for the night. I stay in the justly famous Grand Hotel.

Mackinac Island is a beautiful place with restored old homes all around and within its village market area. Some homes sit against the hillside, looking out over the harbor, with Fort Mackinac as their massive neighbor. It is a fort started by the British and later added on to by the Americans. Its purpose was to guard the Straits of Mackinac and keep the enemy out of Lake Michigan. Today, it is not all that impressive a structure, but it's kept up nicely and serves as a minor tourist attraction. The Island has one curious feature: it allows no motorized vehicles on its streets. Transportation is by foot, bicycle, or various horse-drawn conveyances. A few people choose to walk, but not many and only for short distances. There are hundreds of bicycles parked in racks or being pedaled up and down the streets by tourists, shopkeepers, and workers in uniform, giving the place something of the air of an Asian city. Horses do the heavy work. They pull taxi carriages and hauling carts loaded with building materials, golf clubs, shop inventory, and everything else that needs to be moved from one place to another. Along the way, the horses leave their droppings, providing employment of sorts for a number of sweepers and adding an unforgettable aroma to the place. It strikes me as ironic that motorized vehicles should be prohibited anywhere in Michigan, the home of Motor City. That they are replaced by horses makes the place seem a time warp, as if the state is somehow ashamed of what the automobile has done to America.

~~~

The island harbor is clear and sunny, there is no wind, the sea is calm, but just off in the distance... fog, again. I am sure it is only a patch, like the one at Detour Passage, but it sits over the long bridge across the Straits of Mackinac, and under this bridge pass many ships. The

VHF radio is buzzing with warnings from this ship or that passing through the Straits. I head out to the edge of the fog bank, right at the bridge, put *Rascal* into a calm spot of water in the lee of a bridge piling, and wait for the fog to lift. A short while later, I see an area of blue sky in the general direction I want to go and head for it. It opens up into clear skies over calm, blue water as I head for the Grey's Reef Passage, a channel through dangerous shoals. These shoals seem to be a threat only to deep-draft boats, but I follow the Passage nonetheless. Once through, we run along the east shoreline of Lake Michigan, stopping briefly in the resort town of Harbor Springs, then overnight in Ludington.

This lake's shore is very different from the shores of Georgian Bay and the North Channel in Lake Huron. Here the coastline is a nearly continuous stretch of massive sand dunes and sand cliffs rising straight off the lake's surface. These cliffs have not the first sign of human habitation. Others are lower and tree-covered. As we head south, homes begin to dot the coastline here and there. Villages along the way can be spotted from the water by the presence of their breakwaters, protecting the harbor from the vicious waves that come with the winter storms. It is after Labor Day, and as if by some universal agreement, the hordes of summer tourists have suddenly disappeared. Hundreds of boats sit idle in their slips, waiting to be hauled out for winter storage before the harbors begin to ice. Restaurants and shops close or reduce their hours. There is a sense that the people are bracing themselves for yet another cold winter. I take the hint and decide not to linger unduly.

The lake remains calm as we make the nearly seventy-mile crossing from the east to the west shore at Chicago. Not a boat or ship comes into sight the entire crossing. As we near Chicago, I expect to see the dramatic skyline but cannot—not at twenty miles out, nor at fifteen, nor even at ten. Finally, at just more than five miles I see a dim outline of massive buildings just barely discernible through the pale, smoky haze that hangs over the city. As we draw nearer, the immensity of the place begins to set in. It's not the height of the buildings, nor their number, that overwhelms. It is the breadth of the skyline, stretched for miles before me all across the horizon. In the foreground, there is a calm, blue, flat surface. It is Nature at rest. But in the distance beyond is Man at work. He works to subdue and control Nature. And these great buildings are elaborate monuments to his success.

We enter the inner harbor and pass through a small lock into the Chicago River. This section of the river, passing from Lake Michigan through the heart of the city, is remarkable. There is no other quite like it anywhere I know of. The river surface is about ten feet or more below the street level above and is bounded on both sides not by shoreline but by vertical concrete or steel bulkheads. The visual effect is like a roofless tunnel—well, not quite roofless, because many bridges, mostly old and rusting, cross the river. There are so many in so short a river span that they form a sort of broken canopy. But the most dramatic sight is the tapestry of giant buildings formed of concrete, steel, and glass that rise up from the river's edge all along its route. It is as though the river were a sunken street passing among and enclosed by these monoliths. We stay the night in an unusual marina sitting alongside the river. It is a cavernous concrete cave carved out from under one of the large buildings. If Batman had a Batboat, this is where he would park

TEN

Big Muddy and Long Ditch
Chicago to Mobile Bay

THE CHICAGO RIVER, after it passes through the center of the city, quickly becomes rust belt industrial. It is lined with hulking, rotting, forlorn industrial plants, tank farms, loading docks, and fuel depots. There is nothing attractive or recreational about this waterway. It is a commercial work area that, on the Sunday I pass through, is resting.

A few miles downstream, the Chicago River joins the Illinois River, where industrial turns agricultural. Instead of dilapidated plants and tank farms, there are equally run-down, abandoned grain elevators and corn processing plants. Mile after mile of them. A few still operate, served by towboats moving barge strings up and down the river. The tiny towns and hamlets along the river, most of them, turn their commercial backs to the waterway, most offering not even a landing dock for passing boats or a ramp for local access. They are oriented toward the fields of corn and soybeans that line both sides of the river. We pass through seven locks along the way from Chicago to the confluence of the Illinois with the Mississippi. These drop the water level in stages from 580 feet above sea level at Lake Michigan to 420 feet at the junction with the upper Mississippi.

At long last, we leave the confining banks of the Illinois and join the mighty, muddy Mississippi at the small town of Grafton, Illinois. After the restricted, winding, unattractive Illinois, the Mississippi is a visual feast. At the confluence of the two, the Mississippi, here at least a half mile wide, begins a big, slow concave turn and, as if to dramatize the turn, the bank is lined with several miles of high, steep, white-faced cliffs at river's edge. It is a powerful river with a current that ranges from four to seven miles an hour. It is wide and turbulent. Its surface is a jumble of currents, crosscurrents, and eddies. There are "pillows" everywhere, rounded patterns of water that indicate an upwelling, a sort of vertical current. As *Rascal* flies across the top, she is buffeted by this surface confusion. She moves from side to side in short, delicate steps, as though she were dancing on light feet upon this the greatest of all our rivers.

At the town of Portage de Sioux, we pay our respects to the inspiring Shrine of Our Lady of the River, who stands solemnly, hands clasped in reverence, watching over the safety of the boats that travel the big river. We stay the night at Alton, Illinois, famed as a center for antiques and, as many towns along the Illinois and Mississippi Rivers, newly revitalized by a gambling casino. Thanks in large part to the tax revenues from the casino, the town has built a fine new marina behind a massive breakwater. The marina where we tie up for the night has floating docks attached to pilings. These must stand high enough to prevent the docks from floating over their top and thus becoming unattached in periods of high water. The enormous height of the pilings is visual evidence of the local experience with the Mississippi's periodic episodes of flooding. A grain elevator at the shoreline in Alton has a red stripe painted on its walls about fifteen feet above street level, with a sign indicating this was the high-water mark on a fateful day in August 1992.

~~~

Just downriver from Alton, on the east bank, sits the town of Wood River. This was the point of departure on May 4, 1804, for one of history's greatest adventures, the expedition of Meriwether Lewis and John Clark. A short distance downriver from Wood River the Mississippi is joined by the Missouri, adding still more turbulence to an already tempestuous waterway. At the point where their currents meet, *Rascal* dances about, pushed sideways, one way and then another, by the confused flow. As we pass through the confluence, we come immediately to a dangerous fork. To the right is the main river channel, wide and inviting, drawing the unsuspecting mariner into a stretch filled with treacherous rocks extending all across the river, often submerged when the river is high. It is called, appropriately enough, the Chain of Rocks. The left fork is a narrow canal, the Chain of Rocks Canal, built to bypass the danger. We take the canal, pass through a lock at its south end, and rejoin the Mississippi.

Here we begin a cruise down the long stretch to Cairo, Illinois and the junction with the Ohio River. The upper part of this section, close by St. Louis, is alive with heavy river barge traffic. Barge strings, as many as ten barges long and six barges wide, are tied together with heavy wire rope or thick hawsers, and the aft-most of these are in turn connected to monster towboats with huge, rumbling diesel engines having up to ten thousand horsepower. When these towboats are pushing hilly loaded barges upriver against the tremendous current, their powerful motors and massive props create huge standing waves up to five feet high. Turbulence from the prop wash extends behind them for more than a mile. These barge strings are an important form of commercial inland transportation, carrying coal, fuels, agricultural products, chemicals, timber, and other bulk commodities required in a dynamic economy.

The Mississippi is not a recreational waterway. It is a working river. For all the romance of its history, from its discovery in 1541 by Spanish explorer Hernando DeSoto, to Mark Twain and Huck Finn to Gershwin's "Ole Man River," the Mississippi remains burly and aggressive. With its tributaries, it goes about its business of draining over a million square miles of mid-America, and the restraints man has tried to put upon its powers have served more to confirm than to constrain them.

We arrive at the Ohio River and pass by Fort Defiance situated on the point of land formed by their intersection. We head east against the current up the Ohio, itself a broad, forceful river, less muddy than the Mississippi. Its shores are lined with verdant forests and show little development other than farming. Nearly fifty miles east of the Mississippi, the Tennessee River joins the Ohio at Paducah, Kentucky. We head up the Tennessee, to the Kentucky Lock, on our way to the Tennessee-Tom Bigbee Waterway.

This is one of the busiest locks on the inland waterways. When we arrive, it is nearly six o'clock in the evening. The lockmaster tells me by radio that there are six northbound towboats with barge strings on the south side of the lock and six on the north side with us southbound. Some of the barge strings are doubles—meaning they are, with the towboat, longer than the lock—so they will have to be passed through in two cycles. The lead half of the barges will be pushed into the lock by the towboat and disconnected; the towboat and remaining barges will back out. When the lock is filled (or lowered, as the case may be), the powerless lead half will be pulled out of the lock by a helpful towboat on the other side or pulled out by a winch system built into the guide walls extending out from the lock chamber. The lock cycle will then be reversed so the trailing half of the string with the towboat can be passed through to connect again with the lead half and be on its way. Finally, after we have waited two hours tied off alongside a barge string, the lockmaster radios to say he has been passing through only northbound boats and now will start working on those southbound. He tells us that *Rascal* and a light boat (a towboat with no barges attached) called *Little Jessica* are to enter the lock immediately behind the then-exiting tow string.

It is now eight o'clock at night and the sky is pitch black. I turn on *Rascal's* red and green navigation lights mounted on the bow and discover they are not working. Probably all the pounding has had its effect. I turn on the white navigation light mounted high on the T-top. It works. *Rascal* is far more nimble than the other river traffic, so if I keep a careful watch, the broken navigation lights should not present danger. As we approach the mammoth lock, the barge string exits slowly. Its captain sweeps the river ahead with a powerful searchlight and fixes it on *Rascal* for an instant to be sure we see him. I flash the white light to acknowledge and move far off to the side of the channel as he passes. Then *Little Jessica* enters the chamber and, when she is secured to the floating bollards on the lock wall, I am instructed to enter the chamber and also secure to a bollard.

At fifty-seven feet, Kentucky Lock has a lift much higher than those we have been through thus far. We are going from low to high, so when we enter, the pool inside the lock is at the bottom, and the massive lock gates are standing open. The walls and the closed downstream gate rise above the pool more than eighty feet around. The pool is 600 feet long and 110 feet across, giving us the visual effect of being a tiny speck floating at the bottom of a canyon. *Little Jessica's* powerful engines, even at idle, send waves of deep bass reverberating throughout the chamber. All around the rim of the lock, eight stories high above, are mercury vapor lamps casting their yellow glow in the blackness of the surrounding night. It is all an eerie scene, as though we were entering the yawning maw of an alien spacecraft. We secure as instructed, tying up to floating bollards built into the lock walls. The lock gates close behind, and the pool becomes a mass of turbulence as it is flooded, lifting us effortlessly to the surface of Kentucky Lake. Into blackness the lock gates disgorge us. The dark of the night is punctuated only by the lights of the waiting tow strings, sitting silently. Using a portable spotlight, and without the benefit of charts, I slowly pick my way across to the side of the lake, locate a channel marker, and enter a marina for the night.

~~~

Kentucky Lake—at 180 miles long, 160,000 acres, and 2,400 miles of shoreline—is one of the world's largest man-made lakes. It is one of nine mainstream lakes on the Tennessee River, all constructed and operated by the Army Corps of Engineers as part of the Tennessee Valley Authority project of the 1930s. It offers more than eighty resorts and marine facilities, the massive Land Between the Lakes recreation project, and every other conceivable diversion. This is the heartland of houseboating. A houseboat is essentially an apartment on a barge.

Spacious and practical but not stylish, they are to the TVA lakes what RVs are to the nation's highways.

We move easily down the wide lake, surrounded by heavy forest and hills, and into the narrower part of the Tennessee River until we come to a place known to the Confederates as Pittsburg Landing and to the Union soldiers as Shiloh. As we pass it, I slow to idle speed, gazing up at the high bluffs where thousands of men gave their lives. After finding a marina late in the afternoon and tying up next to a huge houseboat, I borrow a car and return to the battlefield at sunset. On this quiet evening in the fading light of a fading summer, I walk parts of the battlefield, carefully marked with the positions the two armies occupied on the two days of this terrible fight.

Casualties totaled more than 24,000 men. As I leave the place at dark, solemn, even melancholy, at the thought of such death and suffering, I reflect, as thousands before me have reflected, on what possibly could lead men of the same country to inflict such carnage on each other. Slavery was of course the catalyst but not the cause. A tiny few Confederate soldiers owned slaves. The soldiers never thought they were risking death and dismemberment to enable a few planters to own slaves. The war itself was begun, though neither side wanted it, by the incoherent bungling and incompetence of politicians. At the most fundamental level, however, the war was a clash of two dramatically different cultures, the Warrior Culture of the South and the Puritan Culture of New England.

The South, fierce and warlike, excessively proud, with an exaggerated sense of honor, and strongly resistant to central authority, rebelled at what it perceived as self-righteous meddling by the Puritan Culture. The alienation became complete when the South, for the first time since the eighteenth century, lost control of Congress and the White House. Lincoln won with a minority of the popular vote and failed to carry even one of the fifteen southern states. With a diminished political voice and facing the divisive issue of slavery, the South's leaders felt their personal honor required they secede. Though subdued by time and lessened by television and other technological advances that have helped to produce a shared popular culture, the animus between Warrior and Puritan continues, with today's battle-ground being the floors of the two houses of Congress, particularly the House of Representatives. It is there that the almost uniformly conservative, anti-statist South, whose home is now ironically in the Republican Party, the party of Abraham Lincoln, continues to assert the values of its unique culture.

~~~

We have crossed almost the full north-south length of Tennessee on Kentucky Lake and the Tennessee River. Passing through the Pickwick Lock, we enter Pickwick Lake and a short distance later we find the unobtrusive entry into the Tennessee-Tombigbee Waterway. The entrance lies within the embayment of Pickwick Lake, which forms a common boundary of Alabama, Mississippi, and Tennessee. The Tenn-Tom Waterway is 253 miles long, linking the Tennessee River with the Tombigbee River. The Tenn-Tom is joined at Demopolis, Alabama, by the Black Warrior River, and the combined waters then flow into Mobile Bay. From the Tennessee River to Mobile Bay, the entire proj-ect is 470 miles long. This undertaking, the largest ever completed by the Corps of Engineers, was finished in 1985 at a cost of two billion dollars. Not counting the Pickwick Lock on the Tennessee River, there are twelve locks on the entire length of the system, dropping the water level 341 feet to Mobile Bay. The thirty-nine-mile northernmost section, called the Divide Cut, linking the Tennessee and Tombigbee Rivers was built by moving more earth than was required to be moved for the Panama Canal. The Tenn-Tom is five times larger than the Panama Canal and has a lift three to five times greater.

Controversial from the beginning, the Tenn-Tom project is a fine example of what happens when money is pork-barrelled among com-peting uses by politicians. It gets spent not as it would in the private sector—on the project that promises the highest risk-adjusted rate of return and thus enhances net wealth—but on the project whose supporters have the most political power. It thus enhances the elect-ability of the politicians and benefits a few at a cost to many. As a commercial waterway, the Tenn-Tom is a failure. Barge traffic is marginal and, of course, far below the rosy projections political supporters used to sell it. Most traffic is small recreational boats moving from one fishing spot to another or snowbirds on bigger pleasure craft traveling north or south seeking better seasonal climate.

The waterway is not without its benefits. One of these is that it offers a wonderful opportunity—actually twelve wonderful opportunities—to memorialize one politician or another. Recently, for example, the inelegantly named Aliceville Lock and Dam, named for a nearby town, was rechristened in honor of one of Alabama's Congressmen, who was particularly adept at spending other people's money. He was one of the politicians who managed to get it spent, of course, on the Tenn-Tom, thus bringing modest, temporary improvement to the local economy. The structure now assures the immortality of Congressman Tom Bevill. Conventional memorials are usually dedicated after the memorialee dies. However, in the current fashion for politicians, Tom Bevill's immortality is assured even before he passes to the Great Beyond—in fact, even before he retires. And there are eleven more of these memorials-to-be just waiting for new names.

Another benefit of the waterway is that it offers an opportunity for regular, taxpayer-subsidized socializing. Actually, it offers two. There is the Tenn-Tom Development Authority and the Tenn-Tom Development Council. Should two such closely related agencies seem redundant, one need only consider how many more political appointments, paid staff, and advisory committees two such entities make possible rather than merely one. There are the inevitable annual retreats, typically held at fine resorts. These offer the chance for all those who benefit from the waterway project at taxpayer expense to continue to do so over many years.

The trip down the Tenn-Tom is uneventful. Unlike the riproaring Mississippi, the Tenn-Tom is a slack water passage; there is virtually no current. Neither is the waterway susceptible to the forces of wind, given its narrow width and banks on both sides. Marinas and overnight sleeping accommodations are few and far between. I spend more nights aboard *Rascal* here than in the rest of the trip combined, four nights in all.

As we leave the waterway through the Black Warrior River and enter Mobile Bay, darkness is almost upon us. As dusk turns to night, we head out across the bay and reach a small town whose felicitousness matches its name, Fairhope, Alabama. Founded in 1894 by Utopians, its government adhered to the single tax theory espoused by the philosopher Henry George. Essentially, this called for the community, through the town government, to own all the land and lease it to its citizens. The stream of rental income would thus replace the variety of taxes customarily paid by citizens in other towns. If the value of the land increased, it was thought to have increased solely due to the advantages conferred on it by the community. The increase in value was thus thought to belong to the community and was expropriated by an increase in rent. As with Oglethorpe's utopian scheme in Savannah, this one also proved unworkable.

Despite its flawed beginnings, this tiny gem of a town flourishes today. It may be the only town of its size with a full-time horticulturist. Even the tops of the sidewalk trash cans are planted with flowers. The town sits high on a bluff above the eastern shore of the Mobile Bay. It is graced by massive pines, broad, spreading oaks draped with Spanish moss, and an abundance of flowering shrubs and flowers of all kinds. Its commercial buildings are quaint; its graceful houses look homey and lived in, not massive or opulent. The people of Fairhope are warm, polite, easy-going. The manager of the town marina where *Rascal* is docked offers to lend his shiny 1984 Chevy El Camino pickup truck to a complete stranger—me. Delighted, I accept and use it, carefully, to tour the town in grand style. I think what a very nice place this is. For those who like small towns, it would be hard to improve on Fairhope, Alabama.

ELEVEN

The Redneck Riviera
Mobile Bay to Key West

AT THE SOUTH END OF MOBILE BAY sits Fort Morgan, guarding one of the two channels linking the bay with the Gulf of Mexico. It was into this channel on August 5, 1864, that Admiral David Farragut led a fleet of Union ships intent on disrupting the Confederate blockade runners who used Mobile, along with Wilmington and Charleston, as a haven for their activity. He also wanted to destroy a new Confederate iron-clad, the CSS *Tennessee*, recently built in Selma and moved down the Alabama and Dog Rivers to take up position on the north side of Fort Morgan, just inside the bay. Farragut elected to enter the bay through the channel guarded by Fort Morgan, but his task was complicated by pilings the Confederates had driven into one side of the channel, forcing the invader's ships to run a gauntlet close under the guns of Fort Morgan. To make matters worse, the Rebels had planted a field of submerged explosive devices, today called mines but then torpe-does, in much of what remained of the channel.

Farragut's column, with four ironclads and fourteen wooden war-ships, sailed into the narrow opening between the torpedoes and the beach in front of Fort Morgan. The lead ironclad, disregarding orders to stay in the cleared part of the channel, ran into a torpedo, which exploded and sank the ship, blocking the channel. The rest of the col-umn was then brought to a halt in point-blank range of Fort Morgan's guns and was being badly mauled, including the flagship, *Hartford.* Farragut, lashed to *Hartford's* mainmast rigging for a better view of the action, knew in the days before, under cover of darkness, his men had removed many of the torpedoes and found others to be duds. As a Southerner, I like to think that Farragut owed some of his skill and outrageous daring to having been born in Tennessee. Faced with the alternatives of playing sitting duck, retreating, or running westward through the torpedo field, he issued his now-famous order, "Damn the torpedoes. Full speed ahead!"

The shot-up column got through the channel only to be confronted by the *Tennessee* and three gunboats. Badly outnumbered and outgunned, the Rebel gunboats were quickly dispatched, leaving only the *Tennessee*. Sometimes in combat, bravery and reckless self-abandonment merge in acts of startling heroism. Such an act was Farragut's "damn the torpedoes" order, with the Admiral himself lashed to his rigging like a target. Another occurred when the *Tennessee*, alone in the face of an overwhelming enemy, mounting just six guns, attacked the Union force of seventeen ships and 157 guns. In forty minutes, it was over. The *Tennessee*, without steerage, losing power, with most of her gun ports jammed closed, ran up the white flag. Farragut and the Union ground forces then turned their attention to Fort Morgan, which was besieged on August 9 and, utterly devastated by thousands of artillery rounds from ships and shore, surrendered on August 23, 1864. Over the very waters where all of this took place, now calm on a balmy late summer day, *Rascal* skims along, her captain thankful nobody is shooting at us.

The Gulf Intracoastal Waterway (Gulf ICW) travels more than a thousand miles through five states. From Brownsville, Texas, at the Mexican border, it hugs the Gulf Coast all the way to San Carlos Bay at Fort Myers, Florida. Most of its length is made up of the protected waters of rivers, bays, and canals. There are, however, two long sections of open water, from Lake Pontchartrain to Mobile Bay through the Gulf of Mississippi, and from Apalachicola Bay to Tarpon Springs through the Gulf of Mexico. We enter the Gulf ICW where it passes across the mouth of Mobile Bay, along side Fort Morgan, and turn east, passing through Bon Secour Bay, Wolf Bay, part of Perdido Bay, across the mouth of Cotton Bayou, and along the north shore of Ono Island. The land is covered in pine trees standing gracefully amid a blanket of wiregrass and palmetto below, here and there a hammock of live oak draped in Spanish moss. Much of the shoreline is pristine uplands gently washed by warm brackish water lapping on white-sand beaches.

We are less than twenty miles now from my boyhood home, in rural west Pensacola. We stop at Perdido Key and tie up at the private dock behind the home of Pete Cicchine, just off the Gulf ICW on Old River. Pete is there to greet us and welcome me to his home for a few days of rest and repairs. We have been good friends since we first met at age ten. We went our separate ways for a while, but in recent years have reestablished a close friendship. After attending but never graduating from college, Pete went to work selling folding cartons for a major paper producer. He sold to plants all over the country, who used the cartons mostly for consumer foods such as frozen chicken, fish, and shrimp. He worked hard, learned the business, and got to know the people in it, especially his customers. After ten years of this, Pete saw an opportunity. Small customers, those with orders too small to meet the minimum order size of his employer, were being badly served by manufacturers of small cartons. He thought he could do better, and he yearned to work for himself. He chafed at the corporate hierarchy. Pete took out a second mortgage on his home, used his savings, and with every nickel he could find, scraped together enough to buy a tiny, broken-down, rusted-out tin shed in a remote Alabama town and enough machinery and supplies to begin producing his own cartons for the small customers.

It was a lot tougher than Pete had thought it would be. In the early years, he operated and repaired the worn-out machinery himself, purchased the paper board, ink, glue, and other supplies, called on his customers, trained employees. He did nearly everything, worked hundred-hour weeks, slept in the plant, drove himself relentlessly. He was operating on a shoestring at first, barely making payroll each month, always on the edge of financial disaster. Nevertheless, he persevered and slowly began to make progress. From virtually nothing, Pete built a business that today sells nearly ten million dollars of folding cartons annually and is the dominant firm in its market segment. It is a reliable, low-cost supplier of specialty folding cartons and small packages all over the country. It provides secure, full-time employment to many people in a small impoverished town where Pete's people would otherwise likely be unemployed. Pete, a Falstaffian character with a sybaritic love of life, now lives comfortably in his beach home, where he practices his first love, restoring and collecting old Porsches, and his second love, living well. He presides over his company's major decisions and monitors its performance daily, but he leaves the routine management to people who have been his loyal employees for years and with whom he shares the profits. Now in his mid-fifties, he is a contented man and a good friend.

The part of the Gulf Coast extending roughly from Fort Morgan at Mobile Bay on the west to Apalachicola on the east, is known by its habitues, with pugnacious defiance of conventional standards, as the Redneck Riviera. This is a region of vintage Warrior Culture. It was here that as a youth I fished, hunted, drank, caroused, loved, felt pain and elation, sang, danced, fought, raced, laughed, and cried. I did not work (much), study (at all), pray (except not to get caught), obey (either the law or my parents), or live virtuously, as a Puritan youth might. It was a fine place to grow up. Temptation was never far away. It was the place, in short, where I became inducted into the Warrior Culture. Here, too, just up the beach at Gulf Shores, Alabama, is where singer and songwriter Jimmy Buffett did the same, more or less, in his early years.

If there is a defining institution on the Riviera, it surely is the Flora Bama Lounge and Package Store, where they play the hardest. Located right on the beach at Perdido Key, sitting astride the border between Alabama and Florida, the Bama was in the early 1960s an unpainted, ramshackle affair of indeterminate age with a pot-holed dirt parking lot and seedy interior. Fortunately, little has changed. It was and is where adolescents seek furtive beers among the unlawful, thus irresistible, pleasures of the place. It is home to the annual Mullet Toss, in which saturated adult white males, otherwise sane, attempt to throw a slimy dead fish as far as they can. It is also home to the hugely successful annual Country Music Song Writers Festival, a week-long celebration of old and new country music.

Pete and I, in veneration of our heritage, visit the Bama, listen to soulful country music, and watch the boisterous, irreverent crowd, wearing an amazing array of tribal uniforms. There are shaggy-haired, bearded, pot-bellied bikers and their buxom babes; dirty-denim-clad, hard-core rednecks with their snaggle-toothed girlfriends; shaved-headed, trim, Boy-Scoutish Navy pilots fawned over by pre-Junior League coquettes husband-hunting; hopelessly yuppified college fraternity and sorority kids in rigidly correct designer outfits; and aging rakes courting portly, halter-topped, multi- divorced wild things. Pete and I feel right at home. The Surgeon General's report on the dangers of smoking is not taken seriously here, nor are admonitions about high-fat diets, especially the fat contained in boudin ("boo-dan"), the spicy Cajun sausage. These are sensory people for whom play is far more important than work, and they are masters of play. Pete and I manage to leave before we are played out, and even before closing time.

After saying a fond goodbye to my old friend, we move out into the Gulf ICW, under Perdido Key bridge, and into Grand Lagoon. We pass by the handsome home and dock of Jackie and Earl Robinson. He is my very good friend, also since age ten, with a long interruption after high school. Pete and I had tried to visit Jackie and Earl, but couldn't locate them on this trip. We supposed they were out fishing, as they like to do most weekends. I regret not seeing my friends on this trip but I'll see them again— soon, I hope.

Rascal runs smoothly along the north shore of Perdido Key State Park, which is the eastern tip of the Key, eight miles long and less than a half mile wide. The park is all pure white rolling sand dunes, marked here and there by stands of scrub pine or clumps of grasses. Its south coast on the Gulf of Mexico is one of the whitest beaches anywhere, and its north, washed by the quiet waters of Grand Lagoon, is productive habitat for great blue heron, snowy egrets, ibis, horseshoe crabs, blue crabs, sea trout, and much more. As we leave the Grand Lagoon, we cross the inlet that joins the deep harbor of Pensacola Bay with the Gulf. On one side of the inlet sits the stone bulwarks of Fort Pickens. Occupied and held throughout the Civil War by Union forces, it very nearly was the site of the war's first hostile action, losing the distinction to Fort Sumter by just two days. Its garrison spent most of the war in comparatively harmless artillery duels with Confederate installations nearby.

On this clear, warm day the modest skyline of Pensacola can be easily seen across the bay off our port beam. This is the City of Five Flags. It changed hands seventeen times, being at one time or another under Spain, France, England, the Confederacy, and now, of course, the United States. Its first settlers were among the earliest European settlers of the New World, preceded only by a Spanish effort on the Georgia coast in 1526. On August 14, 1559, a Spanish fleet of thirteen ships entered Pensacola Bay, carrying soldiers and civilians whose mission was to establish a permanent settlement. They were led by Don Tristán de Luna y Arellano. What they established was anything but permanent. After starvation, a hurricane, desertions, and near mutiny, the last of the settlers were rescued from Pensacola's shores.

Cruising these same shores, the waterways of my youth, we pass through Santa Rosa Sound, past the beach resorts of Navarre Beach, Fort Walton Beach, and Destin, and along the fabulous beaches of St. Andrew State Park at Panama City. The Gulf ICW east of here narrows to a scenic passage on canals, creeks, and rivers through palm-covered swamp, pine forest, oak hammock, and near tropical jungle. About sixteen miles from Apalachicola Bay, the channel opens wide to form Lake Wimico, narrows again, then joins the strong-flowing Apalachicola River, where we turn south until we come to its mouth at the town of Apalachicola. Here we pass under the John Gorrie

Bridge, named for the man who arguably did more for the development of Florida than any other person: he invented the precursor of modern air conditioning. He lived in Apalachicola and died here a pauper, unable to convert his invention to profit.

We cruise east along the St. George Sound, remaining in the lee of St. George Island and Dog Island, then head out into the open Gulf of Mexico for an unprotected passage across the Big Bend area of Florida, setting a course for the west coast at the mouth of the Suwannee River. The wind is blowing hard out of the east across the very shallow Gulf. Seas are nasty. As we near the Suwannee, we gain lee protection, and the seas abate. Here, however, there are shoal waters even ten miles offshore, requiring much vigilance. We turn south along the west shore of Florida on a course that will take us to Anclote Key, just offshore from Tarpon Springs. The shoreline does not suggest a Florida beach. For mile after mile, the dense swamps of this region, once the home of Seminole Indians, reach to the very edge of the Gulf. Collapsed palms and oak and pine roots, shorn of earth by relentless tides and pounding waves, line the water's edge. There is little beach, only shallow water lapping at the fallen trees.

Quite unlike most of Florida's coast, here there are no homes to be seen. No structures of any kind. Only dense, impenetrable, dark swamp punctuated by an occasional oak hammock, a tidal marsh, or wiregrass savannah. The waterfront is accessible only by water or the few old two-lane macadam roads that run laterally from Highway 98, reaching to St. Marks, Keaton Beach, Steinhatchee, Cedar Key, Yankeetown, Crystal River, Homosassa Springs, and Tarpon Springs. The low coastal area of the Big Bend is drained by a series of jungle-like rivers, flowing black tannin-laden water. The Ochlockonee, Wakulla, St. Marks, Aucilla, Econfina, Fenholloway, Suwannee, Waccasassa, Withlacoochee, Crystal, Homosassa, Chassahowitzka, and the Anclote are only the principal rivers. There are others.

I locate the narrow, winding entrance channel into the Withlacoochee. It begins four miles offshore, and outside its boundary are exposed oyster beds and sand flats where shorebirds wade. As we enter the deep, narrow river, a sign warns that this is a habitat for the manatee, and we must slow. There are endless miles of waterway in Florida, where manatees may chance to roam, designated as slow-speed zones. Manatees are harmless vegetarians, ponderous, blubbery mammals, something like large, fat seals, with a paddle-shaped tail. About three thousand of them (the exact number is unknown) roam Florida's rivers and estuaries, surfacing to breathe, then submerging in search of food. Occasionally, though no one knows how often, they are struck by the propellers of speeding boats and, on rare occasions, they die from the injury. As it turns out, the manatee is almost perfectly adapted for life among modern humans. It is both harmless and adorably ugly. These attributes assure that it will be passionately embraced by those who profess to love animals in a way that they could never love, say, alligators. Gators, every now and then, eat people and pets and, as a result, get bad press. The result of the manatees' charm is many miles of slow-speed zones. There are no slow zones for gators.

The Withlacoochee is filled with diving anhingas, cormorants, graceful ospreys, elegant, long-legged blue herons, and more. The tide has pushed saltwater about a mile up the river. Playing along the discernible tide line is a large school of small bottle-nosed dolphins. They are jumping, porpoising, chasing schools of baitfish onto the shallows, and seem to be having a grand time. We arrive at the dock of the rustic Izzac Walton Lodge in Yankeetown, where I stay the night. The town was founded in 1923 by members of the U.S. branch of the Izzac Walton League, the environmentalists of the time. The original owner of the Lodge was a Yankee and was so called by the locals. The name stuck to the town. The Lodge was built as a place from which to launch nature excursions into the surrounding area. The town is today not much to look at, but the Lodge has been nicely restored and has a very good restaurant. Nature tours are available, but not the kind where hundreds of camera-toting tourists, laden with environmental angst, load onto a huge boat emblazoned with "Eco-Tours." Here, one steps onto the rear deck of an outboard-powered converted mullet boat, sits in an aluminum lawn chair, and putt-putts into one of the truly magnificent wilderness areas left in Florida.

As we leave Yankeetown, we cruise effortlessly south along the coast to Anclote Key, a small island just offshore from Tarpon Springs, then past the gleaming white sands of Three Rooker Bar and Honeymoon Island. Here begins a long stretch of dense, ocean-front development that stands in stark contrast with the shoreline we have just traversed. We pass along Clearwater Beach, Indian Rocks Beach, Treasure Island, and St. Petersburg Beach, jammed with high-rise condos and hotels, commercial shops, gracious mansions, apartment houses from the 1950s and 1960s, and modest homes. Finally, we enter Tampa Bay, as did Pánfilo de Narváez in 1528 and Hernando de Soto in 1539.

Narváez seems to have been a man naturally given to bad judgment. Promptly upon arriving by ship near Tampa Bay, he and his three hundred men and forty horses set off overland near the western shores of Florida toward modern Tallahassee. This was yet another of Spain's relentless, if entirely understandable, quests for gold, preferably already mined and smelted, there for the taking from those who owned it. He complicated his task and discomfited his men unduly by sending away his ships with their cargo of food and supplies and, no doubt, more importantly, the wine and women. He directed them vaguely to an alleged harbor to the north where ships and troupe would rendezvous. The ships, loaded delightfully with all the good stuff, found a harbor and cruised the area looking for Narváez. We are left to wonder just how assiduously they searched. This went on for a fun-filled year before the ship returned to its home port in Spain without Narváez or his men. Meanwhile, the intrepid Narváez discovered that the Apalachee Indians could become hostile when mistreated, with unpleasant consequences for him and his men. Eight years later, four lone survivors, not including their leader, found their way to Mexico City to tell the story of the troupe's amazing misadventures.

Next came the redoubtable de Soto. He launched his expedition from Tampa Bay with more than six hundred soldiers and their retinue, determined not to repeat the errors of Narváez. After aimlessly wandering about much of what is now the southeastern United States, fighting constantly with Indians along the way, the survivors, half their original number and again not including their leader, returned to Tampa Bay more than four years later. They had traveled 3,700 miles, found no treasure, but managed seriously to annoy almost all of the natives.

Determined not to repeat the mistakes of my predecessors in Tampa Bay, I treat the natives kindly, though most are from places like New Jersey and not, technically speaking, natives. St. Petersburg, where I stay the night, is an improved city. The average age of its inhabitants has declined to something less than forty, down from the days when it was known as "God's Waiting Room." The city still suffers intermittently from a bad press that will in time, no doubt, be replaced by a more accurate portrayal. Its city center, situated on the bay, is nicely restored with fine marinas and hotels, parks, and shops. The manicured tropical landscape, blowing gently in the sea breezes, lends lush color to an already colorful place.

Leaving Tampa Bay, we head south on the Gulf ICW through Sarasota Bay and the modest retirement town of Venice. There *Rascal* is closely approached by a lone dolphin, sticking its head out of the water with open jaws anticipating the free fish that locals apparently feed it. We are a disappointment, so it returns to patrolling the waterways looking for handouts from other boats. We leave the waterway at Venice Inlet for the open Gulf to be free of the monotonous manatee zones, and run close along the shore, passing beautiful beaches lined mostly with single-family homes and a state park where flora is left undisturbed for all to enjoy. At Gasparilla Island, named for the apocryphal pirate José Gaspar, we visit the enchanting island village of Boca Grande and the delightful old Gasparilla Inn, both clinging doggedly to the 1950s. Playground for the rich and famous, Boca Grande has something of the old money feel of Palm Beach. Here tycoon J. P. Morgan died at his estate in 1913.

This island marks the north end of one of the most scenic bodies of water in Florida, the Pine Island Sound, ending at Point Ybel on the south end of Sanibel Island. Into this body of water flow the Myakka and Peace Rivers, reaching their confluence at Charlotte Harbor, adjoining the north end of the sound. Separating the sound from the Gulf is a chain of tiny barrier islands. These begin with Gasparilla Island at the north end, followed by Cayo Costa with its completely untouched state park, surely one of the prettiest islands anywhere in the world. Next is rustic and unattached North Captiva, and the tastefully done but overdeveloped Captiva and Sanibel Islands. These last two stand as evidence of what happens when isolated, primitive islands close to a growing city are connected to the mainland by a bridge. I spend a delightful evening at the charming Tween Waters Inn on Captiva. East of these islands lies the main body of the sound and east of this, its namesake, Pine Island. Much of the water here is quite shallow, the bottom mostly sand. The result on a sunny day is a pastiche of greens and blues, set off against the pure white beaches and a sky that seems joined at the horizon with the rich cobalt blue of the Gulf.

The Myakka and Peace rivers, particularly the Peace, drain the vast savannahs of south-central Florida. Their "valleys," if anywhere in South Florida can be a valley in the conventional sense of the term, form thousands of acres of lush grasslands ideal for grazing huge herds of cattle, which, as it happens, is what they are mostly used for today, when not planted in citrus or mined for phosphate.

Florida's cattle industry had its beginnings with the early Spanish. They brought with them from Spain a rangy, long-horned, unusually dim-witted but hardy animal. Some of these *vacu*, the Spanish term for cow, escaped into the forests and swamps and, predictably, multiplied. After almost three hundred years of multiplying, there were a lot of stray cows wandering around Florida. By the mid-1800s, the early pioneers began to gather these cows into herds, pulling them out of the palmetto thickets, swamps, and pine forests and collecting them on the open grasslands, at first to eat and later to sell. Ironically, they found a ready market in Cuba among the Spanish, who paid in gold coins. To deliver these cows, the early cowboys drove them over the vast grasslands, often through the Peace River valley, to the shipping point at Punta Rassa at the mouth of the Caloosahatchee River. This spit of land today is the point of departure for the causeway and bridge to Sanibel Island.

~~~

Since arriving at Anclote Key, just north of Clearwater, we have had the option of using the Gulf ICW, protected from the Gulf by a string of barrier islands, or, on calm days, running in the Gulf itself. As we head south from Fort Myers and Sanibel Island, we no longer have that option, except for a short stretch at Marco Island. We will be exposed to whatever the Gulf has to offer, and on this day it is unpleasant. As we head south out of the lee protection of Sanibel Island, we are greeted by four- to five-foot waves slamming against the starboard bow. After some trim adjustments, we settle in for an uncomfortable passage to Marco Island. There we enter Big Marco Pass and the maze of deep channels winding through mangrove islands. Were it not for the Coast Guard-maintained channel markers, we would quickly become lost in this thicket of look-alike islands.

We exit the protected waterway at Coon Key on Gullivan Bay, just behind the Cape Romano Shoals, and head south along the west edge of the Ten Thousand Islands. Here we enter the region brought wonderfully to life by Peter Matthiessen in *Killing Mister Watson* and *Lost Man's River*, both novels about life and death among the brigands, scofflaws, and fugitives that inhabited these islands in the early years of the twentieth century. This cluster of dense, dark, mosquito-infested islands stretches along the southwest Florida coast from Cape Romano to about Pavillion Key, a distance of twenty-five miles or so, and extends seaward from the mainland for about five miles. Most of this area lies within the boundaries of the Everglades National Park. On a nautical chart, this impenetrable maze of chaotic, helter-skelter growth looks as if it were a magnified cross-section of a vital organ. We make for Indian Key Light, then turn east through Indian Key Pass, winding through the labyrinth with the benefit of channel markers until we reach the forlorn village of Everglades City. This swampy hamlet, once a center of illicit drug smuggling, has been the home of the Rod and Gun Club since the 1920s. Built by the southwest Florida landowner and developer Baron (his first name, not a title) Collier, as a private hunting and fishing lodge, visited over the years by Presidents and other notables, it is today a slightly seedy hotel and restaurant. Mementos of its history, along with a handsome collection of stuffed dead animals, adorn the paneled walls of its lobby and maintain the hunting lodge ambiance.

We depart the Ten Thousand Islands and find the mouth of the Little Shark River, which we ascend from the Gulf. This, along with the Shark, blarney, Lostmans, Huston, Broad, and Roberts rivers, drains the Everglades across the southwestern shores of Florida into the Gulf. A marked channel leads to Oyster Bay, where it joins the Everglades Wilderness Waterway, a tortuous water path of inter-connected creeks, bays, and rivers from Flamingo on the extreme southeast coast deep into the Everglades, exiting at Everglades City. The Park Rangers warn that boats longer than eighteen feet or with high windshields should not attempt the waterway. *Rascal* flunks on both counts, so we avoid it in favor of a leisurely cruise up the Little Shark at idle speed, turning the motors off now and again to enjoy the peaceful, natural splendor of this dark, primitive place.

Leaving the Little Shark, we cruise along the extreme south shore of Florida, a long stretch of uninhabited, remote white-sand beaches, called Cape Sable, and then set a course for Key West. Our course takes us first across the shallow, pale green waters of Florida Bay to Vaca Key, where we intersect and join the Intracoastal Waterway. The ICW channel follows closely alongside the Seven Mile Bridge of U.S. 1 at Marathon, then winds its way among shallows, sand banks, and patches of mangrove, across luminescent green waters through the Bahia Honda and Big Spanish Channels, before reaching out into the Gulf. As we leave the protected waters, heading almost due west, the wind picks up, blowing out of the east, driving waves at our starboard quarter. I drop the trim tabs a few notches and increase the throttle in a moderately successful effort to stabilize *Rascal* against the sloppy seas.

Our destination is the sea buoy marking the entrance into the Northwest Channel leading through the shallows into Key West's harbor. We skirt the edge of a labyrinth of keys, shallow banks, and mangroves. The charts show the depth here is fifteen to twenty feet, plenty of room for *Rascal,* whose hull draws only about three feet off plane, and two feet on. The water is murky, stirred up by the wind and waves, making it hard to tell shallow from deeper water. I watch the depth gauge carefully. At last, in building seas, we reach the sea buoy and turn up the channel toward Key West. As we enter the harbor past a spoil island now being developed as Sunset Key, we pass Mallory Pier, the sundown party place and about all that's left of this part of the once raffish waterfront. We dock in a small harbor alongside a Navy pier.

TWELVE

Wreckers and Developers
Key West to Jacksonville

WHEN THE EARLY SPANISH first came upon this place, it was littered with the bones of the losers in a battle between warring groups of Indians. The Spanish called it Cayo Hueso, Island of Bones, which the English, always eager to corrupt someone else's language, corrupted to Key West. It is the westernmost of the Florida Keys connected by rail and road, but not the westernmost of the Keys. That distinction belongs to the Dry Tortugas, a small group of tiny islands eighty miles farther west in the Gulf, forming the tail end of the geographic comma that punctuates South Florida.

Early on, Key West seemed an unpromising place. It was hot, dusty, and covered with scrub brush on soil incapable of supporting much that was edible. It was remote and could be reached only by sailing vessels over treacherous waters. Prosperity, it seemed, was an unlikely prospect. Then one day prosperity did come, washed up on its shores, literally, in the form of cargo from the holds of wrecked ships. It was then that local entrepreneurs realized what a truly bountiful place Key West could be, the result of a fortuitous combination of conditions. Key West is at the end of a long chain of coral reefs reaching down from Miami. Alongside the reefs flows the powerful Gulf Stream as it heads east then north through the Florida Straits. Ships northbound steer a course in the center of the stream to get the maximum benefit of its flow. Those southbound, steer along the extreme landward edge of the stream to minimize its effects and catch southwest-flowing eddy currents. This course brings the ships perilously close to the reefs.

Navigation in those days was, to put it generously, approximate. Nautical charts were often unreliable, storms frequently struck the area, particularly in late summer, and lighthouses did not exist. In short, Key West offered everything one could hope for to operate a thriving salvage business—and thrive it did. A boom in shipping brought tons of assorted valuables crashing onto the nearby reefs, all to the delight and handsome reward of Key West wreckers, as they were called. When a ship was spotted foundering on a reef, a fleet of wreckers sailed to the site as fast as the wind would carry them. The first to arrive was designated Master of the Wreck and received a disproportionate share of the prize. The wreckers then gathered up the treasure and returned to Key West, where it was auctioned. They took their generous cut from the auction proceeds or by taking payment in kind. Undertakers and lawyers had long known there were profits to be made from the misfortune of others. Now the enterprising citizens of Key West turned their forlorn little island into the wealthiest town in the United States, thanks to other's misfortune.

Even wrecking had its ups and downs, however. Dependent as it was on Acts of God, the appearance of wrecked ships on the reefs was a chancy thing. Weeks, even months, could pass without a profitable tragedy. Things got worse as navigation instruments and charts got better. Thus, the enterprising wreckers figured out how to lend the Almighty a helping hand. They strung a rope between two donkeys, hung ship's lanterns from the rope, and walked the animals along the beaches at night, leading passing ship captains to believe they were seeing floating vessels. Thus, enticed onto the reefs, the ships delivered up their cargo to the imaginative wreckers of Key West.

Alas, not even imagination could postpone the inevitable. Navigation instruments and charts continued to improve. Lighthouses were built along the great chain of reefs—over the strenuous objection of the wreckers. And ships began to be built of iron.

The wonderfully prosperous wrecking business began to dwindle and with it the economy of Key West. It never again saw such fabulous riches as washed ashore in the glory days.

After attending to yet more repairs on *Rascal's* now disturbingly unreliable motors, I wander about town for a few days, taking in all the requisite tourist stops. I talk to a dropout, an aging hippie, two bikers, a stranded yachtie, a blue-collar auto mechanic turned real estate salesman, and a lesbian politico. There seems to be no end to the palette of colorful humanity that finds its way to this place.

The afternoon before we are to leave, I indulge myself in one of the many sensory pleasures of Key West and its tropical waters. Aboard *Rascal*, I idle out of the harbor onto the shallow flats west of the bight, out beyond other boats, where there are no people around. The water is calm. I turn off *Rascal's* motors, allowing her to drift with the gentle tropical breeze. I set up a swim ladder off her stern and throw a line into the water, one end secured to a cleat, and swim naked in the warm waters, savoring the experiences this journey has brought to me. Before me, the sun drifting slowly toward the horizon paints the sky a rich and changing tableau of pink and orange. A full moon has risen out of the soft gray eastern sky and is suspended just above Key West's skyline. With a setting sun in the west and a rising full moon in the east, I am doubly feted by Mother Nature. She and I have often been on opposing sides in this long voyage. This evening she seems to wish to make amends.

~~~

But not for long. The early morning brings strong easterly winds—twenty-five miles an hour or so. We leave the bight in the lee of the island of Cayo Hueso and head toward Hawk Channel. As we round the southernmost point of the United States, a popular tourist attraction, located at twenty-five degrees, thirty-two and seven-tenths minutes of north latitude, we run headlong into nasty five- to six-foot waves. I drop the trim tabs to their maximum setting, forcing the bow down, and advance the throttles to add still more pressure on the bow. *Rascal* slices through the onrushing waves, sending great sheets of white spray billowing into the wind. We are several miles offshore on the Atlantic Ocean side of the Keys, in twenty to thirty feet of water in Hawk Channel, which runs between the Keys and the long line of dangerous reefs that have sunk so many ships along their entire length. This channel extends the length of the Keys from Key West east and north in a great arc to its terminus at Fowey Rocks near Miami. We pass Stock Island, Boca Chica, Saddlebunch, Sugarloaf, Cudjoe, Summerland, Ramrod, Big Pine, and Spanish Harbor Keys. When we reach Loggerhead Key, I change course and make for the Bahia Honda Bridge, passing under it into Big Spanish Channel on the Gulf side and into calmer waters on the lee side of the islands. We are now back in the Intracoastal Waterway.

Here the ICW is dangerously shallow outside the marked channel and I pay close attention to my piloting. This is no place for short-cuts, even with *Rascal's* shallow draft. We pass by Vaca Key, Upper and Lower Matecumbe Keys, then historic Indian Key. Here, in 1838 during the Second Seminole War—there were three—a force of some three hundred Seminoles attacked and massacred nearly all the inhabitants. Continuing, we wind through narrow creeks lined with dense mangroves, then cross open sand flats over shimmering, pale green waters in shallow bays. We cross Blackwater, Barnes, and Card Sounds before reaching the open waters of Biscayne Bay.

At the north end of the thirty-mile-long bay, we come into view of one of the most spectacularly beautiful skylines anywhere. It is Miami, one of America's few truly international cities. Rising out of the clear green waters of the bay, set against the deep blue of the tropical sky are dramatic office towers, colorfully whimsical, avant-garde condos, a lively waterfront shopping area, and, nearby, massive, gleaming cruise ships preparing to sail. All of this is surrounded at street level by stately royal palms, colorful bottlebrush trees, graceful seagrapes, and banyans. Off to starboard is Key Biscayne, protecting this end of the bay from the Atlantic Ocean, and to port is Coconut Grove and

Dinner Key. We pass under the bridge of the Rickenbacker Causeway, where the channel takes us along the banks of Brickell Avenue and its exhibition of modern, aggressively exuberant, iconoclastic buildings, past the mouth of Miami River and Brickell Key, chockablock with massive condo projects sloping back from the water in the style of Aztec temples. As we leave the city waterfront, it seems as if we have passed through a wildly colorful, three-dimensional landscape painting.

The area to the north of Miami, where we are now cruising, is a densely populated, intensively developed, narrow stretch of ICW that continues more than eighty miles to Jupiter Inlet. This stretch is often not wider than a highway and almost entirely lined with concrete or steel bulkheads. On most weekends it is packed with hundreds of powerboats. Their collective wakes, with no place to dissipate, rebound off the bulkheads, making for a very bumpy waterway. With idle-speed zones, both for safety and manatee protection, it is slow going, like driving eighty miles over pot-holed roads through a residential area at five miles an hour.

This part of Florida's coast, from the south end of Miami north to Palm Beach, is called the Gold Coast. Perhaps more than any other part of Florida, it is the result of large-scale real estate development dating back to the land boom of the early 1900s. It was all preceded by the audaciously aggressive and visionary genius Henry Flagler with his railroad and hotels. Then, John Collins and Carl Fisher bought large parts of a scrubby mangrove-encrusted island in the 1910s and on it developed Miami Beach. In south Miami, George Merrick developed the Mediterranean-style community of Coral Gables, with its distinctive architecture, lush tropical landscaping, and an imaginative commercial district. North of Miami, Joseph Young developed Hollywood while Addison Mizner lured the wealthy to Palm Beach and Boca Raton. These were projects on a grand scale, rising out of sandy scrub lands, fueled by easy money supplied by compliant bankers. With a massive influx of tourists and new residents seeking relief from grim northern weather, Florida boomed and property prices exploded.

It was one of the great speculative bubbles of all time and, like all periodic bouts of collective madness, it ended in calamity. A railroad strike in 1925 caused travelers to avoid Florida. A hurricane in 1926 reminded newcomers of the risks of living here. New migrants stopped coming and residents moved out. Property prices collapsed. Banks failed. Thousands of people who had thought of themselves as newly rich were now newly poor. In 1928 two thousand of them became newly dead, thanks to yet another dreadful hurricane. And to this litany of disasters was added the Great Crash of the stock market in 1929, which simply kicked dirt onto the grave of the Florida boom. It would not be until after World War II, nearly twenty years later, that Florida would recover from this devastation. Yet, here we are today, cruising the waterways dredged by these early developers, admiring the still magnificent homes, grand hotels, and shopping areas they created. The millions of people who congest the area today confirm that it remains as desirable a place to live as the early developers had dreamed. I spend the night in Ft. Lauderdale, at the Marina Marriott Hotel, on the Intracoastal Waterway across from Pier 66 and its ever-present collection of the world's great yachts.

As we leave the beautiful emerald-green waters of Jupiter Inlet, the banks of the waterway recede from the channel and once again are lined with mangroves, palms, and tropical shrubs. We are passing through the Hobe Sound National Wildlife Refuge and, just north of that, the St. Lucie Inlet State Park. These are home to abundant species of birds that seem to go about their daily business unmindful of passing boats and nearby development. Osprey shriek from their huge nests high in the treetops, great blue herons walk with regal posture on spindly legs along the shallow flats, and snowy egrets perch on the lower limbs of mangroves and upturned tree stumps. We leave this enchanting scenery at the junction of the ICW and the St. Lucie River. Off to starboard is the treacherous St. Lucie Inlet, an often difficult passage into the Atlantic, safely undertaken only with recent local knowledge. To port is the mouth of the St. Lucie River. A boat heading west up the St. Lucie, as I have done, through its south fork and into the St. Lucie Canal can reach and cross the mammoth Lake Okeechobee, exit the lake on the Caloosahatchee River and arrive at Fort Myers and Pine Island Sound on the Gulf. The route, officially known as the Okeechobee Waterway, crosses the Florida peninsula at nearly the widest point, is 156 miles long and passes through five locks and under more than twenty bridges.

Our journey takes us north on the ICW past Jensen Beach, Fort Pierce, Vero Beach, then through the Pelican Island National Wildlife Refuge. From Stuart north, the ICW is a marked channel passing through more or less the center of the Indian River. Not a river in the conventional sense, it is typical of the bodies of water sandwiched between the Florida mainland and the long, narrow chain of barrier islands that begins with the small islands along Biscayne Bay near Miami and extends, with few interruptions, all the way up Florida's coast and north to New Jersey. The barrier islands are separated here and there by inlets connecting the ocean with the inland waters. Tides flow through these inlets, periodically flooding and draining the rivers, bays, estuaries, and lagoons that line Florida's coast. The tides mix the ocean's salt water with the fresh water flowing eastward from the many rivers that drain the swamps and savannahs of Florida's uplands.

As we leave the serene beauty of the Pelican Islands at Wabasso, the waterway widens noticeably. It becomes a long, straight, open passage, several miles wide, crossed frequently by high bridges or power lines, its shores lined with small, quiet towns like Sebastian, Melbourne, Eau Gallie, Rockledge, Merritt Island, and Titusville. We pass the high gantries of the Kennedy Space Center standing incongruously above the flat, green coastal marsh. The huge Merritt Island National Wildlife Refuge surrounding the NASA launch facilities occupies nearly all of the eastern shore of the river, extending eastward to the ocean. Its 25,000 acres harbor eagles, pelicans, blue and white herons, vultures, ibis, egrets, and more. At its north end, the Indian River makes a big, sweeping turn to the east. Outside its channel are numerous tiny, sand spoil islands with a variety of scrub growth, guarded on this afternoon by a coterie of wading birds. In the deeper water nearby, pelicans are dive-bombing for fish, their kamikaze-like plunges sending sheets of white spray exploding from the water's surface.

The Indian River at this point runs headlong into a narrow stretch of land that is part of the mainland shore that extends south and widens considerably to form Merritt Island. This would be the end of the Indian River were it not for a law passed during Teddy Roosevelt's administration authorizing the first project on what would later become the Intracoastal Waterway. That project was to dig a narrow canal across this stretch of land and link the Indian River, then the northern terminus of the inland waters reaching down almost to Miami, with the Mosquito Lagoon, the southern terminus of inland waters extending far to the north. The canal was dug at a place where Indians had for centuries hauled their canoes between the two waters and is today called the Haulover Canal. It is a lovely if short waterway, lined by dense Australian pines, with white sandy shores and calm, green water. At its eastern end, it opens onto the wide expanse of the shallow, primitive-looking Mosquito Lagoon, part of the Canaveral National Seashore.

Once through the Haulover Canal, the ICW channel turns sharply to port amid a cluster of small fishing boats anchored in and near the channel. I keep *Rascal* off plane in order not to rock these boats with her wake. After we're through, I throttle up to planing speed, and *Rascal* leaps ahead, breaking through the light chop kicked up by the afternoon sea breezes. The channel runs close alongside the west shore of the Lagoon. The shoreline is a picture of Florida as it was centuries ago. Small islands lie between mainland and channel, covered by palm and palmetto, their shores lined with pure white sandy beaches. Here and there the beaches protrude into the shallow green waters to form spits and bars. In the distance are shallow lagoons, beyond them the semitropical jungle of the mainland. With hardly any imagination at all, it is easy to see the ancient Indians paddle their cypress dugout canoes over these waters in their unending search for food. The search goes on today, but dugouts are replaced by outboard-powered fiberglass boats with electronic fish finders, and bone-tipped spears with an astonishing array of rods, reels, line, and tackle. It is not clear whether the moderns catch more fish.

As we leave the green waters of Mosquito Lagoon, the channel hugs the mainland coast. To starboard is a dense maze of mangrove islands and shallow, winding salt creeks, most lying within the Canaveral National Seashore. A five-mile section of this channel is a designated manatee zone, where all boats are required to travel at slow speed, about five miles an hour. The zone is largely ignored by the local boats. We continue on through New Smyrna Beach, past the Coast Guard Station and the Ponce de Leon Inlet. On this windy day, the ocean side of the inlet is a wall of thundering white breakers. Big rollers crash through the protecting line of jetties to menace smaller boats inside the inlet. This was once one of Florida's deadliest inlets. Here a long list of ships were grounded, pulverized by the relentless pounding surf, their passengers and crews often drowned. The *Vera Cruz* in 1880 was the inlet's most famous victim and one of Florida's greatest maritime disasters. She grounded in a storm while bound from New York to Havana and was broken apart by a huge wave, killing seventy-one of her passengers and crew. In 1887, a lighthouse was built that still stands and is open to the public. Later improvements were made that helped but did not tame what locals called the "Killer Inlet." Continuing north, we enter Halifax River, another of the many nonrivers that line the east coast of Florida, separating mainland from barrier islands. It is wide and shallow most of its length, beginning at the inlet and continuing through Daytona Beach north to the Tomoka River. Like all these nonrivers, this one is tidal, salty, and more accurately described as a lagoon.

Florida's history, like that of most of the United States, is a history of commercial adventure by bold men of heroic vision and grand, if flawed, deeds. Entrepreneurs—like Flagler, Plant, Merrick, Mizner, Disston, Yulee, Collier, and others—pursued massive real estate projects and built railroads and bridges that formed the early infrastructure of modern Florida. But these developers were long preceded by perhaps the boldest, if not the most spectacularly successful, profit-seekers of them all: the early Spanish kings, principally Carlos V (also known as the Holy Roman Emperor, Charles V) and Philip II. Spain, like all countries of Europe at the time, pursued mercantilist, beggar-thy-neighbor trade policies, designed to accumulate gold and silver in the royal treasury. Because of its habit of getting caught up in long and costly wars, Spain's treasury was forever in need of replenishment. The most effective way to fill empty coffers was to take the stuff by force from people that already had it but were not strong enough to keep it. The New World, primitive as it was, offered a splendid opportunity for such exploitation.

Of course, conquering people and taking their treasure was itself costly, and risky, too. The problem for the Spanish Crown was how to reap the potential rewards while shifting both the cost and risk to others. Spanish royalty solved the problem by using a contractual arrangement that modern lawyers would call a joint venture. It was sheer genius. The Crown offered primarily three incentives. The first, a nearly universal practice among governments everywhere, was a grant of monopoly, in this case, exclusive rights to a specific territory. The second, also common among governments, was the grant of titles of distinction, providing upward social mobility by taxonomy. The third, all important to the pious Spaniards, was assurance they would be welcomed warmly into the gates of heaven. These inducements the Crown would bestow upon promising adventurers mostly from the ranks of the military, a wise choice given the nature of the task at hand.

In exchange, the Crown got quite a lot. Although the terms varied widely, commonly and most importantly the soldier of fortune put up all or most of the money to finance the venture. He also staffed, organized, and led the expedition. In short, he risked his own life, the lives of his troops, as well as his fortune, for a slim chance at fame, title, and greater fortune. Considering the monumental odds against success, this was something less than a desirable bargain when calculated rationally. Columbus had only recently discovered the New World—he did that by colliding with it while looking for a place many thousands of miles farther west. Navigators of the day knew latitudes reasonably well but longitudes were wild guesses. And who knew what warlike savages might be lurking in these foreign lands? Add to these risks the widely prevalent threats of disease, famine, and storms. Yet, in spite of what seemed quite an unattractive arrangement, there was no shortage of intrepid men eager to sign up. Had I lived in that time, I might well have been one of them.

Among the earliest who signed up were the men who explored—exploited is the more accurate term—South America, Central America, and Mexico. Men like Hernán Cortés in 1519 and Francisco Pizarro in 1532 became immensely wealthy from their share of the shiploads of gold, silver, and jewels looted from, respectively, the Aztecs and Incas. The success and acclaim they received at home understandably stirred the passions of others. The prospect of handsome reward was too much to resist so, as we have seen, Don Tristán de Luna y Arellano, Pánfilo de Narváez, and Hernando de Soto, among others, sailed off in a fruitless search that rendered the former bankrupt and the latter two dead. Such is the lust for wealth and glory that not even these misadventures could deter Pedro Menéndez de Avilés. Although he hoped less for gain from gold than from the more prosaic farming, timber, and shipping, he, backed by the wealth of his partners, entered into another of the clever joint venture contracts, this one with Philip II.

Upon arriving in Florida, Menéndez promptly attacked a French fleet at the St. Johns River, just seventy miles north of where we are now, then moved south to found St. Augustine, America's oldest permanent European settlement. The French launched a counterattack by ship that was foiled by yet another hurricane. Sensing opportunity, Menéndez attacked and easily captured the French Fort Caroline on the high bluffs above the St. Johns River. Survivors of the wrecked French ships gathered themselves along the coast south of St. Augustine and marched north toward the St. Johns. They were halted by a strongly tidal inlet, the same place where *Rascal* now cruises slowly. There they met Menéndez, who tricked them into crossing the inlet with his help. On the shore of the other side of the inlet, Menéndez had nearly all the French executed. France, of course, was Spain's competitor in the New World and its enemy but, perhaps more importantly, these French were "Lutheran heretics," that is, Protestants, thus Menéndez, in the peculiar logic of the time, was serving the Lord. To this day, the inlet is called Matanzas, the Spanish word for "place of slaughter."

Things began to go poorly for Menéndez. Four years after founding St. Augustine, he had to apply to the Crown for a subsidy. The thriving business based on agriculture and trade that he hoped for ran into one setback after another and finally collapsed. Menéndez died just nine years after setting out with high hopes for profitable rewards, another in the line of Spain's New World real estate developers come to naught.

Just a few miles farther to the north, we enter the ancient town of St. Augustine. We are on the Matanzas River (yet another nonriver), a part of the ICW, and pass under the draw span of the antique Bridge of Lions. Off to port, just beyond the west end of the bridge, is a cool, quiet, oak-covered park that serves as something of a town square (though here it is a rectangle). Beyond the park is one of Henry Flagler's early creations, the sprawling, Moorish, asymmetrical Ponce de Leon Hotel, now reborn as Flagler College. Designed by the same architects who later designed the New York Public Library, the hotel was in its time the most luxurious anywhere. It still boasts an extraordinary collection of stained-glass windows done by Louis Comfort Tiffany. North of the bridge, sitting at the end of the old town's seawall and promenade is the low imposing fort, the Castillo de San Marcos. Built of coquina, a resilient mixture of seashells and limestone quarried nearby, it replaced nine wooden forts that had been burned by the English or simply rotted away in the steamy Florida weather. It was perhaps the single most important structure of Spanish Florida, and on this bright, breezy day we pass under its guns with considerably greater ease than did the ships of the English, who twice sought unsuccessfully to capture the place. We slowly round the north end of Anastasia Island, now dense with modest homes and 1950s-era motels, but in 1740 the site where James Oglethorpe mounted cannons in the second of the two failed English attempts to capture the impregnable fort. Before us, on a direct line with the fort, is the St. Augustine Inlet, a marked, if shifting, passage protected by jetties to seaward.

Just to landward of the inlet, we turn north up the ICW for the final leg of our journey now three months long. I have called Kitty, to tell her of our arrival. She and Grant will meet me at *Rascal's* home port in just one hour. I am filled with conflicting emotions. This voyage has been all that I hoped it would be. We have met interesting people from very different cultures amid widely varied landscapes. We have confronted nearly all that Mother Nature could throw our way. There were warm, calm, sunny days; days with fierce winds; cold, gray, depressing days; days enshrouded with dense fog; days of inexplicable, impenetrable patches of fog surrounded by transparent blue sky. We have cruised happily over warm, blue, peaceful seas; anxiously over flat, glassy, cold, black seas; fearfully over malevolent giant rollers; monotonously over confining, winding canals and rivers. We have fought terror and panic in the grip of the monstrous standing waves of the St. Lawrence.

I have met briefly some of the people who collectively drive our country forward, the risk takers, visionary people with a mission, the people who create jobs, see opportunity, and, above all, act. These encounters have been uplifting. I have seen three vastly different cultures: the Warrior Culture of my native South, the Puritan Culture of New England, and the Euro-Socialized Culture of eastern Canada. Passing among them, if only briefly, has allowed me to compare their folkways, to see first hand some of the best and worst of each.

The landscapes I have traversed have been widely varied. There were the low coastal plains, salt marshes, and oak and pine uplands of the South; the flat, alluvial plains of the Delaware Valley; the sand dunes and stands of short leaf pines in New Jersey; the rocky, intricately serrated shores of New England; the heavily forested, untouched coast of Nova Scotia; the grandeur of mammoth cliffs plunging to the sea at Cape Breton; the gently rolling red clay soils of bucolic Prince Edward Island; the sheer granite mountain faces of the Gaspé Peninsula; the steep, green hills that line the St. Lawrence River's western reaches; the fjord-like Saguenay River; the sheer rock bluffs of Quebec City; the rocky, spruce- covered islets of the Thousand Islands; the chaotic, rocky maze of the Georgian Bay and North Channel; the high dunes of Lake Michigan; the dull, plowed, flat fields of the Midwest and inland South; the sparkling blue waters and white sand of the North Florida Gulf Coast; the dense coastal swamps of Florida's Big Bend; the emerald-green waters lapping quietly against white sand on the lower west coast of Florida; the dark jungle of the Everglades; the mangrove and coral of the Keys; the dense human development of Southeast Florida; and, just now, back to the salt marsh and pines of North Florida. It has been a kaleidoscope turning slowly, over time and great distances.

There are places where I wish to return to spend more time, places like the upper Maine Coast—Downeast, as they say—Cape Breton, the Gaspé Peninsula, the Saguenay River, Quebec, Pensacola, Key West. There are places I will not make an effort to revisit: anywhere on the Illinois River or Tenn-Tom Waterway, New York City, the New Jersey coast. Still, I am glad I could see them on this trip.

Through everything, it has been *Rascal* and me. My boat, this "inanimate" object, has entered a very private place in me, a place reserved for friends and loved ones. I know every inch of her. I know how she acts and feels in the best of times and the worst of times. She has always been there for me. I am joined to her by bonds of affection.

If I have come to know *Rascal* better, I have come to know myself better, too. As I planned this voyage, there was no doubt in my mind that I could do it. I had seen it more as an adventure than a test. Yet I have been tested: what I am, what I am made of, what I can do, and how well I can do it under extreme conditions. All have been tested. Now I return to what is, perhaps, an even more challenging test—that of everyday living.

Separation from my small family for such a long time has been the worst of it. Though we talked on the phone most days, I missed some early soccer games, missed our dinners at home together, missed the embraces of wife and son. The routine of life onboard *Rascal* replaced the routine of the home, and it will take some adjustment, compromise, to leave the one and reenter the other. Life at sea has been free from most of the subconsciously accepted constraints imposed on us by friends, rules, conventions, and the community standards that we live by. Living within these once again should come easily because years of civilizing self-restraint are not forgotten in three months. But, I have to confess, the adjustment will come reluctantly and with mixed emotions. The nearly perfect state of individual freedom afforded by the open ocean—as distinguished from the regulated confines of the ICW— is an alluring siren. I know it is temporary, and largely an illusion, but its appeal is genuine. It has been drawing men to sea for many centuries, and now I am among them. Shore duty won't be quite the same.

At long last, after three wonderful months, I pull into home port, greet the dockmaster, guide *Rascal* gently into her slip, secure the dock lines, and step out onto the dock and into the arms of my little family. It's good to be home again.

Statistical Summary

Total distance traveled (statute miles) 7,661
Total engine hours 326
Gallons of gas consumed 6,522
Miles per gallon 1.17
Gallons per engine hour 20
Total gas cost $10,412
Average cost per gallon $1.60
Gas cost per mile $1.36

About the Author

PHILIP B. PHILLIPS, JR., 53—called P.B. by friends from his youth and Phil more recently—was born and raised in the country outside Pensacola, about as far west in Florida's panhandle as one can get without running into the Perdido River and Alabama. Barely avoiding reform school, he finished—that's all that can be said of it—local public schools and Florida State University. He served, involuntarily, two eventful years in the United States Army, grew up in the process, and earned an MBA from the University of Miami, and a law degree from Florida State University, where he was an editor of the law review. After some tedious years practicing law, he founded and still owns Phillips & Company, a privately-owned developer of suburban office parks. Since 1974 he has resided in Jacksonville, where he lives on the banks of the St. Johns River with Kitty, his wife of twenty-five years, and Grant, their ten-year-old son. When he is not enjoying the Bahamas, where he and Kitty are building a second home, he is busy planning his next venture: traversing most of the west coast of North America from Anchorage to San Diego, again in *Rascal*. After that, it's anyone's guess what comes next.

CPSIA information can be obtained
at www.ICGtesting.com
Printed in the USA
BVHW040948181121
621927BV00004B/58